GREY FAMI
By: Karen

MW01172099

Printed in the United States of America

First Printing, 2013

Re-edited by: LJ Thomas, 2014

Cover Design by: Shannesha Eacholes

Back Cover by: Asoral Publishing

In Memory Of My Sister

Deborah Neal Green

March 31, 1961 – November 28, 201

God took you so soon, but he always knows best. It is our faith in him that gets us all through these holy tests. Though we may not understand his reasoning at the time, he never makes mistakes, but unfortunately for us, it does not stop our heartaches. Our lives have never or will ever be the same since you have been gone, but by the grace of God we somehow remain strong. I never knew a pain like this could be so great, often times shedding enough tears to fill the great lakes. From the depths of our hearts, we miss you dear love, but God needed you far more in the Heavens above. I miss you my dear sister, this feeling I cannot hide, but I shall see you again one day, on the other side.

Acknowledgements

I give thanks to first of all God the Father Almighty. Without him, I know I could never walk the path he has prepared before me. He continues to keep me strong when I can't find strength on my own. He gives me hope, when all hope has gone. May you add a special blessing to these words and allow them to surpass even my most extraneous expectations.

To that special ear and heart that helped me to see that this is my time to shine because God said so. Your love of God inspires me to the fullest.

To My Son thank you for understanding when Mama just couldn't pull away from this project and thank both you and your dad for the understanding of Mama staying up all night.

To two of the most important people in my life, I know you had your doubts about this dream of mine coming to fruition, but I also know that it came from fear of me letting you down as I know I have done before. I thank you two for making me into the young lady I am today and without you, Tommy and Joe Ann, there would be no me.

Sandy Barrett Sims, you did a great job on the first edit of Grey Family Preys. I guess too well because when I decided to re-edit this second edition; I had to find another editor. (Psst, I had her busy on other projects). I thank you for always having my back, even when we are ready to take each other heads apart.

LJ, you came to me highly recommended by one of the best in the Lit world, Dion Cheese whom took it upon his self to mentor me as he took me under his wing and asked nothing in return except performance in my work. He gave me a 3.5 on the first edit of Grey Family Preys, but he did so with advice. He extended a helping hand to new writer and his wisdom is gratefully accepted. Dion I took your advice and created an already good book into an even better book.

GREY FAMILY PREYS

PROLOUGE

It was early October and the weather was still nice enough for the kids to be riding their bikes around the neighborhood while grills were going with leg quarters, hotdogs, burgers and the famous southern barbequed ribs. There was a lot of loud laughter and plenty of shit talking going on all around Dell Drive on this chilly October evening. Reece was among the ones talking shit, laughing and having fun, but that came to a halt when he took notice of something the others around him were oblivious to Reece saw the bubble shaped Chevy circle the block a few times and the last trip around

Reece figured that even though he was in a small town, something didn't feel right about the car driving by slowly.

"Yo G, I'll hollar at y'all a little later man." Reece said as he looked up the road to see if the car was still in sight. Reece had only recently moved to the small town of Thomson, but had became friends with Bryson Grey, also known as "G". G, along with his brother Tyga and cousin Flex were well known in the community because of the famous dogs that they bred.

"Alright man, come through tomorrow, you know we'll be over this way the same time tomorrow." G said as he gave Reece a dapped handshake.

Just as Reece got onto the bike to peddle into the path that lead through a thin wooded area behind the run-down neighborhood, a shadowed figure illuminated through the street lights. Reece thought it was one of the locals, but as he got closer to the figure, he realized there was something familiar about this person. The hood came off and the face that Reece saw caused him to piss on himself. He tried to turn the bike around and head in the other direction, but the Chevy he had seen circling was now stopped with the windows cracked and each crack produced an AK-47. As fire erupted from the guns, people started running for cover, leaving plates of food behind. G was yelling for his brother and cousin to get down with fear they would get hit. No one knew whom the shots were meant for but G.

Tyga and the other guys quickly pulled out their guns and started blasting in the direction of the car. They were so busy busting shots that they never noticed Reece's execution, but Flex witnessed the entire scene with fear he had never known. The Hooded figure approached a terrified Reece as he dropped the bike and got onto his knees to plead for his life, but there was no pleading his case. The Hooded assassin simply let off 6 to Reece's dome and took off back into the wooded path he emerged from. There were kids playing and riding bikes under the streetlights. There were card games going on, but when the shots were fired bikes were thrown down, cards flew into the night air and doors were being slammed shut and locked, while Reece died on his knees while hands in a prayer position.

While driving down I-20 Kyle was driving as normal as he possibly could, given the state of his nerves and keeping his eyes in the back of him as well as on the side roads. To say that he was nervous would be an understatement. He had tried to set things up so he wouldn't have to get his hands dirty, but the burning of the house in the little back wood town two nights ago didn't work. Kyle thought of the innocent lives he had taken when he had gone like a thief in the night while everyone was asleep and doused the house with lighter fluid. He had put a match to it and drove away knowing that it would burn down before authorities could get there to save anyone, and felt not a touch of remorse. He had been told to make Reece disappear and had gotten word that Reece had beef with a dude up in Warren County. This was the dude's house that Reece had the beef with and figured he would be the first one the cops came looking for. If he could get Reece framed for arson and sent to prison then he knew Reece's days would have been numbered in the pen. He had hoped he could frame Reece for the fire and then sent to prison and when he got on the inside, people that owed him and his crew a favor would have done the deed. This would have saved him the trouble of doing it himself, but his patience and time was running short so he had no choice but to pull the trigger and be sure Reece was totally taken out. Kyle didn't want to face the wrath of his boss for falling short on his job, but he didn't expect to see the face of his best childhood friend.

CUNNINGHAM SCENE 1

The Cunningham small estate sat on 25 acres of land hidden behind hundreds of trees. The only sign of a home possibly being nestled back there was a palatial gate with approved entrance onto the mini estate. The gate had the most unusual colonies on either side of it. They were made of a strange vivid yellow glass. The gate was also made of glass that was a pale yellow. Once you were on the estate, you would take a tree lined scenic route deep into the woods, which opened up to a large 2 acres pond with a gate home that sat 200 yards away. Another 100 yards from the gate home sat their 6,200 square foot home. The home was truly a dream home with four bedrooms, five bathrooms to include a bathroom in each bedroom and a guest bathroom. The master bedroom took up 320 sq. ft. The home also boasted a dining area fit for royalty, breakfast room, kitchen, great room for entertaining guest, and a spacious den for Katrina's alone time as well as a bonus room, which served as a theatre. Katrina Grey-Cunningham had her front porch enclosed and designed for her comfort. This is where she would sit when she was deep in thought and this is where she sat on this evening as she wondered what was taking her son Flex so long to get back into town. She knew they did have shopping malls in the area that he said they were going but dang, he had been gone from the early rise of the sun and it was now high-rise of the moon. While rocking in her chair and indulging in a bottle of Moscato Red, she heard a loud rumbling in the distance that she knew to be her nephew's Mustang 5.0. She just sat there and rocked while reading a book by one of her favorite Authors named Cole Hart. A story called "The Throne" about this Boss chick named Falisa, reminded Katrina of her self. Flex and his two older cousins, Tyga and G, got out of the car and Katrina didn't try to hide the fact that she was upset. "Where in the hell have y'all been all of this Got damn time? Shit I been calling everywhere looking for you boys, and your Granny has called as well. Y'all have worried everybody damn near to death and you all know the family situation with Deb being sick. What the hell took all day and half the night that y'all is just now rolling your behinds up?"

The boys all knew they would catch hell from Katrina and Granny Joe, but they didn't expect to be caught up in a hail of bullets either. Of course they could not share with Katrina the experience that they had endured this day, so they tried to act as normal as possibly and continue to let her think they had truly been out of town all day. "Mama, would you stop all of that cussing, it's not even dark out here good yet." Flex said as he attempted to hug his mother out of sheer relief that he had made it back home alive. He still could not shake the feeling that he knew the guy who had killed Reece. He didn't see a face, but their eyes met briefly and he felt a connection. He also wondered why the guy didn't shoot him when he clearly had the opportunity to do so.

"Well don't give me a reason to be out here cussing about your irresponsible ways and it's close enough to dark. You better be glad I'm not busting all three of your heads to the fucking white meat." Katrina was beyond heated as she stared into each of the boy's eyes and quickly studied their demeanor. She knew they were telling her a boldfaced lie about where they had been, but decided that she would talk with G in private at a later time to get the true story. She knew those boys better than anyone and she saw fear in each of their eyes. "Flex, it would be in your best interest to watch who you are speaking to using that tone of voice," said Katrina to her son as he just shook his head because once his Ma Duke was on a roll there was no arguing with that woman.

G being the oldest of the three tried to diffuse the situation with his Auntie. G was her first-born Nephew, and was a weak spot for Katrina, but not on this evening. "Auntie it was my fault that we were gone so long", said G.

"I don't care who fault it was. All three of you know the deal with your mom." At the mention of his mom, G really began to feel guilty. His mom Deb was his heart and just to think about her illness was painful as it was for the entire Grey Family. Deborah Grey-Simms had once been her family's backbone and she carried that title well. No one knew to what extent she went to ensure that her family was well taken care of until that awful day she fell ill while at work. She had made it look so easy taking care of her family, but Deborah went through hell and her family had only seen the shell of hardship she had to endure in order for her family to function. Deborah Grey and Trevor Simms had been sweethearts for a year before getting married. He was like a dream come true to her until his problem with alcohol and women came between them after the birth of their daughter Bridgette. It had consumed him to the point that his job with Demopoulous Law Firm was in jeopardy and his marriage was quite rocky before the illness of his wife.

Katrina informed them that they all needed to meet at Granny Joe & Pop's, the Grey's home for the family dinner. G, was special in is mom's eyes, because he had been the first-born and he and his mother had a very special bond that could only be shared by a mother and her first-born son. He was an adult with three kids of his own, but after things didn't work out with him and two of his children's mother, he moved back home with his mom and step-dad. G was the product of Deb's first love. Bryson (G) Grey's father had been a walking nightmare and a thorn in the Grey family's side during the courtship of Bryson's parents. Lamont Harris had taken her through hell and would be the first to know the wrath of the Grey family.

MAKING OF KATRINA

Although it was Deborah that lived with Big Momma, it was Thomas and Joe Anne's baby girl that Big Momma took under her wing and began training her at an early age. Big Momma saw something in the young child one day that solidified her hunch that Katrina had it. Big Momma although was a woman of wealth in land, she still went to work in the homes of the wealthy whites. Katrina had taken ill this particular year with Whooping cough and couldn't go to school. Katrina would go with Big Momma to the home of one of the families that she cleaned for while Thomas and Joe Ann went to work in their shop.

The Man of the house always made Katrina feel some type of way and not a good type of way. Katrina would always try to stay right under her Big Momma whenever they were there, but 8 hours on a daily basis made it somewhat hard to avoid the man with the shifty eyes. Mr. McGhee had a son that was only 1 year younger than Katrina and she did enjoy playing with Ralphie. One day while the children were playing a game of hide and seek, Mr. McGhee unbeknownst to Katrina joined in on the fun. She was outside in the perfect hiding place, which was behind the house in some thick he would never find her there.

Katrina heard Ralphie coming her way and covered her mouth to keep him from hearing her giggle. As the feet got closer she became more excited about running out to base and winning the game. Just as she heard the faint crunch of leaves under feet, she leapt out from her hiding place only to be grabbed in a bear hug by a laughing Ralphie. "I won, I won," sang Ralphie. "Now we get to play what I want to play."

"Okay Ralphie, what would you like to play?"

"I want to play Peter, Peter".

"How do you play that game?"

"My dad will show you how to play."

Katrina became afraid and said, "I don't feel like playing anymore. I'm going in with my Grandma." When Katrina went in to help her Grandma with folding laundry, she was sent back outside because Ralphie wanted her to play with him. The rule of the game was, Ralphie would count to fifty while Katrina went to hide with Mr. McGhee. The man grabbed five-year-old Katrina's hand and hid deep in the woods so that Ralphie would not find them. Katrina began to relax because this game was the same as hide and seek. He went on to explain to Katrina that Peter, Peter was a game where she had to find and touch his Peter before Ralphie found them.

"I don't know what a Peter is though," said Katrina.

"Come over here and I will teach you as we go." They came to a clearing where Mr. McGhee could easily see his son running around trying to find them. "Okay, all you do is touch the body part that I call out to you and when you get to the Peter body part, I will give you a dollar after you touch it." The man began with calling out his facial parts, and then as he got to the lower part he called "Peter, Peter."

Katrina just looked confused because she had no idea what this crazy old white man was talking about. Mr. McGhee then unzipped his pants and pulled out his erect penis and guided the little girl's hands to it and instructed her to squeeze it. When he turned to look at Katrina, she had tears in her eyes. "Why are you crying Katrina?"

"I don't like this game, it's scary."
"No sweetheart, it's fun, let me show you." The man sat down on a blanket that he had brought along with him. He pulled little Katrina down into his lap to comfort her until Ralphie could find them.

"I want to sit by myself Mr. McGhee." Said Katrina in a shaky voice.

"Sure you can," he said as he placed her directly in front of him on the blanket. Katrina began to feel a little less afraid until she looked down and saw the man's hand grab her hand and placed it back to that nasty purplish thing between his legs. The terror began in Katrina's life at this moment. He took it no further than that on this day, but there were many days when he would go as far as touching her and telling her that if she told her grandmother any of this, he would fire her and then it would be her fault that

12

her grandma didn't have a job. This abuse would continue for the next year or so and even advancing to the point of Mr. McGhee coming to their home on the weekend just to play hide and seek with Katrina and Geoffrey. Katrina could not understand why nobody knew what this man was doing to her. One day she did tell Geoffrey what had been happening and Geoff was livid, but being only nine himself, there was only so much he could do. One day the man came to play with the kids and on this day he would seal his fate.

Katrina and Geoff were outside their grandmother's home playing, when Katrina looked up and saw Mr. McGhee's old truck pulling up. She began crying and telling her brother that she didn't want to play anymore. Deborah was sitting on the porch reading a book and heard her little sister crying. "Come here Katrina. You do not have to play with that man if you do not want to." Just then Big Momma came out on the porch to greet the man and ask what brought him over on the weekend.

"I just came to play with the kids is all Ms. Sadie.

"Well that's very nice of you to spend time with them like that and I'm sure that they appreciate it."

"But she doesn't want to play with him Big Momma, please don't make her play with him." Deborah said with fear that she sensed and after her brother had confided in her what Katrina told him, she knew that her little sister was scared.

"That's nonsense," said Big Momma as she looked in Katrina's direction and asked her if this was true. Katrina was the only one to see the daring look from Mr. McGhee and she knew what that meant, so she said that she didn't mind playing with him. Deborah knew her sister was scared for some reason and volunteered to play along with them. This made Katrina feel a lot safer until she realized that he might try to do the same thing to her sister. She had to think fast. "Geoff you can count and your sisters and I will go hide," said Mr. McGhee. He never noticed that Deborah had went on down a trail behind the house, but Katrina and Geoff both had seen which direction she went in and Katrina knowing her sister had something planned, played along with it.

"No I want to play a different game, follow me everyone." Katrina said excitedly. They came upon a barn with an old rusty tractor that sat in the front.

As the barn came into view, Mr. McGhee noticed, ten-year-old Deborah playing beside the tractor with her dolls. "Hey Deborah, what are you playing?"

"I'm about to ride into town with my brother and sister."

"We always play this game of a family going into town for grocery shopping. The dolls are my children." Would you like to ride with us Mr. McGhee?"

"Well I don't see why not. This is a pretty old peace of equipment. You have to be very careful on this ancient thing though, it's pretty rusty and could be dangerous." The children then began climbing onto the tractor with Geoffrey and Deborah taking the seats and Mr. McGhee sitting behind Geoffrey on the back tire. He made sure to sit Katrina in his lap and this time unlike the other times, she had a smile on her face.

"Geoffrey, you make sure to watch the road while driving and Deborah you help him watch out for traffic." The sick bastard couldn't wait to put his finger inside of Katrina's small opening. He put his massive right hand under her dress and pulled her panties to the side and roughly inserted his middle finger causing a gasp to escape Katrina's lips that did not go unnoticed by her siblings.

"Okay y'all we will have to stop to let the other people cross," Geoffrey said as he continued on with their pretend trip into town by horse and buggy. He pulled up on the rusty gear of the tractor. The gear pulled back into the tire, trapping Mr. McGhee's left hand between the gear and tire.

"Move that got damn gear boy, shit my hand is stuck you stupid black little fucker". Because the gear was old and rusted, it had the man's hand stuck and all of the pulling was only tearing tissue away from his wrist. Geoffrey and Deborah were in tears laughing, but Katrina however only had tears flowing from her eyes that seemed to have turned a deadly grey. Katrina picked up an iron pipe that she had placed there earlier in the day

14

just for this occasion. She drew back as far as she could and with all the strength her body could muster, she swung and connected with the head of the man that had been molesting her for so many months. He fell from the tractor, breaking his wrist in the process. This brought about even more cries from the man until he looked up and saw the children's grandma. "Ms. Sadie, thank God you're here, these wild monkeys of yours are trying to kill me," the man said just above a whisper.

She looked at all three of her grandkids with disappointment in her eyes. "I know that I taught you all better than this, Katrina give me the pipe baby." Taking the pipe out of her youngest grandchild's hand, she then produced a larger pipe and finished what her grandbaby had started. No one knew what happened that day except the five people there and one trusted man that Big Momma had called about the molesting situation about a week before. No one would ever know what transpired down in that pasture outside of that barn. One thing that Big Momma knew on that day was Katrina Grey was a made person of a different caliber and Lord have mercy on those that crossed her in any way.

DEBORAH'S FIRST LOVE

Deborah Grey had fallen in love with Lamont Harris in the year of 1978 during her junior year of high school. He was her first boyfriend and like many girls with first time loves, she was willing to accept anything thrown her way to be a part of his life. She went through catching him with female after female and heartbreak after heartbreak. She even went through abuse and that was a mistake that Lamont Harris would live to regret. He had not a clue that you just simply did not fuck with a Grey and walk away clean. Ms. Joe, Deborah's mother, had warned him on several occasions but the fool just did not take head to the warnings. Deborah lived with Ms. Joe's mother as a child and into her teen years. Big Mama was a strong woman that had taught Ms. Joe how to be strong as well. Big Mama was also a very smart woman that had buried three husbands and raised three children while running her own farm. She had her own farm on over 200 acres of land back when blacks were still working in the Southern fields of Georgia. Being the smart lady that she was, had afforded her and her three children a very comfortable life. Ms. Joe was her youngest daughter of three kids. When Ms. Joe met Thomas Grey and fell in love the two would marry, but their first-born would remain with Big Mama because she simply adored the beautiful little girl named Deborah. Anyone messed with this little doll of hers was destined to pay, as Lamont Harris would soon find out.

Lamont and Deborah's romance had been bittersweet for her. It was a constant tug of war with the other females in his life, but being that she was blindly in love with him, she endured it all in the name of love. Deborah had the sweetest personality and was loved by all of her friends and adored by her family. The beautiful young Grey girl was envied by lots of girls at her school for her beautiful looks. Deborah was a petite 5" girl that only weighted a buck ten soaking wet. She had smooth skin the color of milk chocolate and a thick luscious mane of hair that reached her shoulders. She was Ms. everything in High School from Ms. Sophomore to Ms. Farren County High. Big Mama made sure that she was the crème de la crème when it came to dressing, as she only wore custom made clothing. Big Momma was an excellent seamstress, and often custom made clothes for the wealthy white families in the area. She often made clothes for Deborah, mimicking the designers Yves St. Laurent and Furstenberg. Whenever she did shop, it would be from the local boutiques.

16

Though Deborah had it all and was clearly royalty in her school, she never looked down her nose at anyone and this is what made her even more special. Deborah fell head over heels in love with Lamont near the end of her junior year in high school. Unbeknownst to most, she was with child when she marched proudly to receive her diploma in the year "79" with the belief that she and Lamont would marry and live happily ever after. Unfortunately for her, Lamont had other plans that did not include a wife and kid. Lamont was the typical pretty boy, tall with skin the color of a lemon with a neat hair fro and believed his yellow shit didn't stink. He was one arrogant fucker that would be knocked of his high horse by a thunder force that he didn't know existed.

Lamont wanted to keep Deborah at bay while he romanced his many women. Deborah being so in love for the first time did what she thought would make Lamont happy. She had no idea that Lamont was out with different women while she was at her home nursing swollen feet and listening to the lectures from Big Mama about putting her dreams on hold for a low life like Lamont Harris. All of the talks Big Mama gave her fell on deaf ears because as far as Deborah could see, Lamont loved her and they would soon be a happily married couple.

Although Deborah had been a straight A student throughout high school, she refused to continue her education for the sake of Lamont. She began to see a different side of Lamont that everyone else already knew. She began getting calls from different females claiming that he was at their home while she was at her home barefoot and pregnant, the truth finally hit her in the face like a ton of bricks. One night she decided to check into one of the accusations while their out of town family was visiting for the weekend. Big Mama's oldest daughter Ruby and her family would visit once a month and Ruby had a daughter also named Deborah and she was known as Big Deb because she was older than Deborah Grey. The two Debs were close in age and were thick as thieves. Whenever Aunt Ruby and her family came home, the entire family would all stay at Big Momma's house and have a fun filled weekend. Big Momma would always cook a feast while her daughters; Ruby and Joanne would catch up with each other. Ruby had a family of six children and four grandkids of her own now. The two Debs and Katrina were inside talking amongst themselves, when the telephone rang. Katrina was the closest to the phone, so she answered, "Hello, hello, hello? "Someone is playing on the phone again," she said as she hung up the phone.

The phone immediately began to ring again and this time Big Deb answered. "Hello, is Deborah there,' a voice said almost in a whisper. Big Deb having an idea what this call was all about responded by saying, "This is Deborah."

"This is Dominique and I just wanted to let you know that Lamont is at my house as we speak. I know that your dumb ass thought he was all yours but you need to know that he has asked me to marry him and I need for you to leave him alone."

Big Deb's nose began to flare as she listened to this bitch on the other end talking all of this shit. "You're the one that keeps calling here hanging up I assume. You must not be too sure that you have him if you have to play little girl games on the phone," Big Deb said heatedly.

"Oh I'm sure that I have him and I was trying to save your silly ass the pain of him breaking up with you, but if you don't believe me you are welcome to come see for yourself."

"Oh yeah. I would love to catch the no good bastard. Just give me the directions and I will be there," the girl never knew that she was not speaking to the Deborah that she thought was Lamont's pregnant girlfriend and had just secured herself an ass whooping. It was on this night that twenty-two year old, Big Deb and Katrina, who was only fifteen at the time but feisty as hell, demanded that they check it out. The bitch had even given them her address, a mistake that she would soon regret.

Big Deb, Lil' Deb and Katrina all piled into Aunt Ruby's 1981 Cadillac and headed in the direction that the female on the phone was stupid enough to give to Deb. When they pulled up to the address, sure enough, Lamont's "79" cutlass supreme was sitting in the driveway. This stupid heifer Dominique actually had the balls to open the door so that they could come in to find a sleeping Lamont knocked out in her bedroom in a sex-induced sleep. Lil' Deb was devastated and ran over to the bed and started raining blows on a sleeping Lamont who woke up startled and fighting back. He didn't realize that it was his seven-month pregnant girlfriend. When his fist connected with her jaw was when all hell broke loose. "Bastard, I know you didn't just hit my cousin," big Deb yelled as she pounced on Lamont and both began giving him the ass whooping of his life. Dominique went to buck and that's when Katrina said, "Oh hell no bitch, you are mine."

Katrina was only fifteen, but she was the feistiest of her siblings and when anyone caused her siblings any harm, they had royally fucked up. Katrina grabbed Dominique by her hair and slung her to the floor where she started raining blows into the young woman's face. Katrina was in a rage because this bitch had been picking on her sister for far too long and where as her sister was meek, Katrina was not. When it came to her family she would become a bitch that no one wanted to cross. Katrina had blanked out beating the girl's head against the floor and grabbing a shoe to smash into the girl's face. Big Deb looked over and knew how Katrina could get carried away and tried to pull her away from the already battered girl. When Katrina became like this it was hard to contain her and as Big Deb tried grabbing Katrina, she then became the target of Katrina's rage. The only thing to calm Katrina was her Big sister pleading for her to please stop and only then did she cease the fighting.

Katrina looked at the bloody Dominique curled up on the floor covering her face and felt no remorse. She then turned her attention on Lamont and looking at the smirk displayed upon his scratched up bloody face, she took a leap with the shoe still in her hand and began wilding out on him. Big Deb held Lil' Deb back as she wanted Katrina to give this low-down dog the beating that he deserved. Big Deb let Katrina get her frustration out a little while longer before attempting to stop Katrina again. That bed was full of blood and Lamont was damn near unconscious when Katrina finally stopped. Katrina stood up over him on top of the bloody mattress and spit on his ass them kicked him for good measures.

"Don't fuck with the Grey family motherfucker or you will find yourself in a fucked up situation," said Katrina. "Don't you ever bring your ass back around my sister again or you can tell your family to get their blacks ready to wear to your farewell affair. Lamont this is not a threat nor a warning, this is a promised fact." She then kneeled down to Dominique and spoke in a calm menacing voice. "Bitch don't even think about calling the fucking cops about this shit that went down here tonight. You called my sister's house and invited this ass whooping into your home with open arms. Now you do have options Dominique and listen real careful so your simple ass will choose the correct option. You can forget this ever happened and never call my sister again or you can call the cops and they can pull the tape of you calling my sister's home harassing her. The last option gives you the bonus of joining me behind bars and getting your ass kicked every single day. I know you will make the right choice because it doesn't bother me

19

which one you choose, I'm only fifteen and was only defending my pregnant sister," Katrina said as she walked out of the room and house satisfied with the damage she had done. Dominique had made the smarter choice and chalked it up to the game. There was something about the way Katrina's voice sounded that had sent shivers down her spine. She didn't want to take the chance on finding out if Katrina was making idle threats or solid promises. Dominique would later leave the area only to visit her family from time to time, but making sure that she never came into contact with the Grey sisters or Lamont again.

Katrina's First

Deborah went on with her life and had a healthy baby boy that she named Bryson Grey. Bryson was the apple of the Grey's eyes and Katrina was especially excited about becoming an Auntie at the age of 16. Katrina and her brother Geoffrey took turns taking care of their Nephew while Deborah would work. Deb was working in a law firm as a Legal secretary and had started dating a young handsome intern by the name of Trevor Dent. One night while Trevor was visiting with Deborah and baby Bryson, there was a knock on the door. Deborah peeked through the peephole and there was Lamont standing on the porch looking as if he was quite upset over something. Deborah excused herself and told Trevor that she would be right back.

As soon as Deborah opened the door, Lamont forced his way in past her and snatched Baby Bryson out of Trevor's arms. Deborah began screaming and ran up to Lamont to get her baby, but he drew his hand back and slapped her so hard that she fell with a thump to the floor. Trevor didn't want to bring any harm to the baby by having a tug-of-war with this fool, but he couldn't come off as a punk either. In one swift move, Trevor grabbed the baby and knocked the hell out of Lamont causing him to go crashing across the glass coffee table. With all the commotion going on, this had awakened Big Momma from her sleep. She had grabbed her 22 rifle that she kept beside her bed and was down the stairs in a matter of seconds and this was good for a seventy-year-old lady. By the time Lamont stood to his feet, the gun was cocked and in his face.

Trevor looked on in amazement at the feisty old lady holding the weapon. Big Momma glared at Lamont and said to Deborah, "Call the police now." Just as she was dialing the phone, her sister Katrina walked through the door. Katrina was about to inquire about whose car was parked out front till she looked up and saw the situation. Katrina's nose flared and her eyes changed into the bluest gray shade that would normally be beautiful. Deborah seeing her sister and the look that she had, knew that this was not going to be good. Katrina quickly took control of the situation. "Deb put the phone down, Big Momma give me the gun, take Bryson and go back upstairs. Trevor, why don't you take my sister to get an ice cream so she can calm down from all of this madness? Trevor didn't think it was such a

21

great idea to leave Katrina with this fool, but Deborah assured him that her sister could take it from there.

After the room was clear of anyone except Katrina and Lamont, Katrina took a seat and assessed the damage done to her grandmother's living room. Katrina was now seventeen and just as beautiful as her sister. They were as different as night and day though. Deborah was the color of milk chocolate standing at only 5'' and weighing 110 pounds. Katrina was a 5'4 honey colored teenager with hazel eyes that changed to the most beautiful gray when she was at her most deadly state. Katrina was stacked to be only seventeen years old and carried her 135 pounds very well. These attributes didn't go unnoticed by Lamont's slimy ass. He sat on the couch as well and began asking Katrina a series of questions about Trevor. "Lamont, Trevor is the last person you should be concerning yourself with," said Katrina. Katrina was patiently and unbeknownst to Lamont, waiting on a phone call from her girlfriend Monica.

Monica and Katrina had been best friends since their junior high school years. Katrina often stayed to herself during her junior high years, preferring not to have anyone in her business. One day while she was walking to class, a group of girls were in the hallway standing beside her locker. 'Excuse me please," stated Katrina. The girls all ignored her and continued to block her locker. "I said excuse me, I need to get to my locker if you don't mind." " Actually we do mind", said one girl. The girl continued to taunt Katrina," We don't see a name anywhere in this area so that tells me that anyone that want to stand here at anytime is welcomed." Katrina only smiled and said, " Yeah, you are right about that Melissa as she walked off smiling as her beautiful gray eyes shined brightly. These black girls think that they are in charge around this school, but have to be reminded from time to time that they need to stay in their lane." Melissa never saw it coming, but she sure as hell felt the powerful blow to the back of her head as her face was smashed into Katrina's locker. The other girls all started screaming when they saw blood pouring out of their friend's face. All of the commotion had gotten the attention of a few kids and teachers that came to the rescue of Melissa. Katrina just went about her business getting her books for her next class and as she was closing her locker back up she was told to follow one of the teachers along with the group of girls to the principal's office. Walking and unfazed by anything that was going on, Katrina followed behind the group of girls and teacher as if she was bored. One of the girls kept looking back at Katrina with a smirk on her face.

Katrina thought, "if this lil' white bitch want it, she can get it too." Mrs. Price, the teacher took the girls all into Principal Smith's office and described the scene that she ran into in the hallway. Mr. Smith took a look at Melissa's face and demanded to know what happened to her. The group of girls all started to point in Katrina's direction and recanting in different versions of what happened. There was one girl that wasn't saying anything. Mr. Smith took notice of this and asked all of the girls to please be quiet as he looked at the quiet girl and asked her what had taken place in the hallway. This was the same girl that kept looking back at Katrina earlier with a smirk on her face. The girl went on to explain how Katrina had tried to get to her locker and Melissa would not get out of her way and then instigated a fight by speaking derogatory remarks about black girls knowing their places. Melissa and the other girls all sat with stunned looks on their faces at the betrayal of their 'friend' but the girl couldn't care less. In fact she seemed to downright enjoy letting the man know exactly what happened. Mr. Smith looked at Katrina and said that he understood how that could make her upset, but that didn't warrant her to take matters into her own hands. He then asked her what would make her do such a horrible thing to another person. Katrina looked at Melissa without an ounce of care and said, " I was simply trying to get to my locker and these bitches refused to move from in front of my locker. I was just getting my books to go to my next class." "She is telling the truth" a voice spoke up. It was the girl that kept looking at Katrina. As I just told you, Katrina was provoked and Melissa has been trying to pick a fight with this girl for weeks now and today I guess she got what she was looking for." "Why thank you Monica for coming forward with the truth and I'm sure that Katrina thanks you as well." Katrina glanced towards this Monica bitch and without taking her eyes off of her, she asked Mr. Smith if she could please get to her next class. As Katrina was walking down the hallway, she heard running behind her and heard the girl defending her calling her name. "Hi my name is Monica," said the girl as she caught up to Katrina. "Thanks for having my back in the principal's office, but I'm late and don't have time for the cheery formalities." Monica was from money and it showed on her lily-white ass just a lil' too much for Katrina's taste. Monica was driven to school daily in her mother's jaguar sporting the latest design wear. Monica decided that Katrina was going to be her best friend and, what Monica Kincaid wanted she always got. Over time Monica accomplished what few could do and that was to become the best friend to Katrina Grey. They became inseparable over time and became known as sisters despite their race. Monica often teased Katrina about having a white grandmother because of her natural straight hair and hazel colored eyes that seemed to change colors right before your very eyes. Katrina and Monica became the best of friends and have a sisterhood that proved to never be broken to this very day. They even started up a business together after working in a chiropractic clinic together and taking it to heights that the doctor never thought was possible. They decided that instead of making someone else rich, why not make them rich and thus the Cunningham Sports clinic was born. Monica's family had their hands in so many cookie jars that they didn't even have to worry about putting but one name on the business as long as Monica was named part owner she was fine with the name. It would prove to be a very smart move on both of the young women behalf.

Katrina's cell phone rang and she looked down at the screen and smiled satisfied that her girl had gotten her text just a little while ago. "Okay are you coming out or just going to sex his no good ass first?" Monica laughed through the receiver. "Sure I can meet you there" Katrina faked a conversation. Katrina disconnected the call and asked Lamont if he could drop her off at a friend's house. "Nah I'm going to sit right here and wait for your sister to get her black ass back here and make sure that fuck nicca don't be coming around my son anymore." Shaking her head back and fourth, Katrina convinced him that wouldn't be in his best interest since he had forced his way into her grandmother's home while having a restraining order to stay away from Deborah. "So Lamont, what's up with that ride I need, will you or won't you let me ride?" Katrina meant to come off as seductive because she knew that Lamont's whorish ass would take the bait.

"Yeah baby girl, I got you. Where do you need me to give you a ride to?" He said while licking his crusty ass lips.

"I'll direct you straight to where I need to go and will pay you for your services."

"That's what I'm talking about right there." As they were walking down the driveway Lamont kept his eyes on Katrina's well-rounded ass and toned hips that had a natural sway when she walked. "I've always wanted to see if you are as good as your sister," Lamont said as he shook his head up and down and licked his lips. "I think you are going to be quite surprised with me." Said Lamont. Your world is about to get hotter than you could have ever imagined." Lamont never saw the look of contentment and smile that crossed Katrina's face as she looked to make sure everyone was in place.

Lamont never noticed the dark color car that pulled out right behind his car. He was too busy thinking about how he was going to get all up in Katrina's tight spot. After driving for about 10 minutes, they passed by a woman trying to flag a car down. Her car was on the side of the road with the hood up. Lamont stopped when he realized that the young lady was alone and was a pretty little blonde. "Hey pretty lady you need some help?"

Monica flashed a pretty smile and thanked him for coming to her rescue. "My car started making a strange noise and then it just cut off," stated Monica.

"Well let me see what kind of noise it seems to make when you start it up?"

"I keep over flooding it when I try," said Monica. If you don't mind, could you please try starting it up for me"?

"Sure pretty lady, I can handle that for you."

"Lamont, I don't have time for you to be captain-save-a-ho right now. I really have better things to do than to watch you try to hoe your ass in this chic's pants." Lamont, never one to let an opportunity to get new pussy get away, looked back at Katrina and said, "Get your ass out and walk then if you can't wait." He never noticed Monica easing over to his car where Katrina was still sitting and talking shit to keep his attention on her as planned while her best friend eased over to her and slid in the driver's seat of Lamont's car. "I'm sorry to hold you up from your trip, but I am grateful that your boyfriend is helping me."

"He is not my man, but he needs to hurry his ass up because I got things to do."

"Katrina just shut the hell up or get your ass out and walk," Lamont shot back as he got in Monica's car and turned the ignition and the car made a stalling noise. He attempted again and while he was trying to start up Monica's car, Monica had knocked his car out of gear and allowed his car to slowly roll backwards. When Lamont tried to start the car a third time, the motor caught on fire and the doors instantly locked. He started yelling for help as the flames began to grow larger. Katrina and Monica had gotten out of his car by now, feeling a safe distance and watched the burning car. Lamont was really getting scared, but wanted to appear strong around the young women but when he noticed that they were just standing there looking at him, he lost his cool. "Why in the hell are y'all just standing there, help me out of this mutherfucker". Katrina and Monica watched as the car burned to a crisp as Lamont beat on the window and his cries for help slowly died down along with his evil spirit. A silent bomb had been installed that was set to go off after three attempts to start the ignition. Monica had to make sure she didn't use any of those attempts while pretending to be in distress because she knew that Lamont would be a sitting duck when the bomb deactivated. "Don't fuck with the Grey family mother-fucker, or you will find yourself in a fucked up situation" Katrina said as she and Monica walked off.

The black sedan that had trailed Katrina and Lamont earlier had pulled up. The back window rolled down and a very handsome white man asked the girls if they were okay. "We are fine daddy," stated Monica. Monica's father Andreas was Greek and like his name, he was a protector to his family. Andreas was in fact one of the wealthiest men in the South, but one would never know this by looking at him and his family. Andreas was the owner of several very lucrative foreign car dealerships and a large construction site that also served as a cleaner for his main source of income. Andreas ordered two of his men to get into Lamont's car and drive it to the garage and properly dispose of it. Katrina was taken back to her grandmother's house and on the way there she thanked her best friend and Andreas for all of their help. "That's what family is for my darling, you are just as much my daughter as Monica is," stated Andreas. When she got back to her grandmother's house, Katrina informed her Big Momma of what had taken place. She assured her that they would never have to worry about Lamont ever again.

"Did you make sure nothing could ever come back to you Katrina?"

"Yes ma'am, Andreas followed me there so everything will be taken care of", Katrina stated as she continued to help with little Bryson until his mother returned.

When Deborah walked in, the first thing she asked was, "Katrina what did you do to Lamont?" Smiling while on the floor playing with her nephew and never taking her eyes off of him she simply stated, "I have to get home, before mama calls over here worried," Katrina never involved her family in anything that she did as Big Momma had chosen her to be the protector because of things that she saw in the child at a very young age. When Big Momma had first learned of the abuse that Katrina was going through, she just made one phone call and that was to Andreas Demopoulous. That one phone call had formed an alliance between two families that would carry on a legacy. The day that Monica came to the rescue of Katrina was no mistake, but Katrina still didn't know to this day that it was all planned. As far as Katrina knew, it was her grandmother that had instilled in her to always protect their family because she was the chosen one to do so. Big Momma had recognized the bloodline that Katrina carried a long time ago. Katrina made sure that her family was safe and she did a good job of eliminating anyone that crossed them. She never wanted them to go through the things that she had with Mr. McGhee all those years ago and she vowed that it would never happen again to anyone close to her.

Geoffrey

Geoffrey ran one of Andreas' construction sites after working there on a trial basis one summer. Andreas was at the Greys' family home one day picking Monica up after spending the day with Katrina. He saw Geoff outside sitting with a group of young guys that he figured were up to no good. Andreas had known the Grey children all of their lives, since their Grandmother had raised him before he went to college and left the area. When he returned as a wealthy man, he never forgot the woman that was more of a mother to him than a nanny. He had asked her if she would help him raise Monica as she had helped raise him. After he had assisted the lady in disposing the body of Mr. McGhee, she would not turn him down. The only condition was, she didn't want her family to know that she would be working for another family after what little Katrina had endured at the hands of that Pedophile. Every since that day, Andreas had become somewhat of protector for the entire family and this day would be no different as he watched Geoff interact with these young boys.

He knew that the boys would be nothing but trouble and he just had to get Geoff away from them. What better way than to put him to work for him and keeping an even better eye on him. He had tried in the past to get Geoff's father, Thomas to come work for him, but the man was too proud to work for anyone other than himself. He did accept a small business loan from Andreas to start up his own business. Thomas Grey started his own garage and though it was not large, it still afforded him the funds to provide for his family. Andreas figured that Geoff was young and just right for training for one of his businesses. He surmised that the reason Geoff was not working with his father was he being young just didn't want to follow in his dad's footstep of becoming a mechanic and having a dirty job. The young generation of today just didn't like getting their hands dirty, literally speaking. He could see the young man as a businessman and like he had been there for the family all of these years, he only though it would be fair to offer him a job in one of his establishments. After all, he had made a promise to their grandmother on her dying bed to always be there for the Grey family, but only in the background. He had been in the background, but often times, he and Katrina would have personal meetings unbeknownst to even Monica.

"Hi Geoff, what are doing with yourself during these long summer days?"

"Just keeping an eye on the girls is all sir."

"How about a summer job with me at one of my construction sites?"

Geoff looked at Andreas as if he had three heads on his shoulders. "No disrespect Mr. Demopoulous, but if I want to get dirty on a job, I could go and work with my dad."

Andreas only laughed and said, "You will not get your hands too dirty playboy," while shaking his head at the young man.

He told Geoff to meet him in his office the next morning and he would see what they could come up with. The next morning Geoff was in Andreas' office bright and early. "So why do you not work with your father Geoff?" I have no interest in working on other people cars, that's just not my style.

"Well would you have any interest in coming to work for me?"

"What do you have in mind for me?"

"I understand that you enjoy working outside, being free so to speak. I have a construction site up in Conyers and could use you there. We could start you off as a site leader and see how you like it.

"Man I think I would love to try it. When can I start?"

Andreas nodded his approval and picked up the phone to tell his secretary that he would be out of his office for the rest of the morning. "Wow, this is a big ass site." Geoff said as he took in his surroundings. All of the large machinery really excited Geoffrey and the only thing running through his mind was *"I'm about to make some bank and come up in rank,"* As they approached one area, Andreas called out to one of his foreman to come over. He made the introductions and told him that Geoff would be his new site leader and to teach him everything that he needed to know. The guy had been with Andreas for twenty years and had proven his loyalty many times. His name was Charles and he took an instant liking to Geoff.

"So you want to be in constructions Geoffrey?"

"Well I'm still trying to find myself, but Mr. Demopoulous said to let him know if it's something that I think I would like."

"Well the first test is to see how well do you know your tools. Give me that brick stretcher over there." Geoff looked around seeing all sorts of tools that he was familiar with, but saw nothing that he thought could be a brick stretcher. Some of the other guys close by began laughing as they saw Geoff searching and pulling tools out of the way as he came up with several that he had never seen and asked if any of those were what Charles was looking for. Geoff had somewhat of a temper and didn't take too kindly to being laughed at. "What the hell y'all laughing at?"

One dude that was not laughing, but had a look of contempt on his face replied, "Looking at your dumb ass trying to find something that is nonexistent".

"Man, who the fuck you calling dumb." Geoff lunged for the guy, but Charles grabbed him by the arm to calm him down.

"Geoff, I was just having a little fun with you buddy. Every new guy gets the same treatment without the smartness from Victor over there." Victor had been working there for five years and was next in line to get the site leader position, so he was feeling some type of way for this new dude to come in off the streets and claim his position when he clearly didn't know shit about construction.

Geoffrey Grey was what one would call a ladies' man standing at only 5'10" and 180 lbs. of pure muscles. He worked out religiously believing that his body is what kept his women wanting more. Geoffrey, like his sister Deborah was a shade darker than their sister Katrina. He had smooth skin the color of milk chocolate and sported a sexy baldhead and a moustache over full lips. Katrina and her brother Geoffrey both were raised in the home with their parents, while Deborah lived with their Big Momma. Often times while their parents were working, Kat and Geoff would discuss how they refused to become victims to anyone ever again. It had taken a long time, but he had learned not to worry about his younger sister because even though she was the youngest, he knew that she could handle herself. He had seen her in action before and had seen a beast unleashed after that day down by his grandmother's barn. But he had witnessed another side of Katrina that other family members had never seen. "He would never forget what he witnessed that horrible night.

Geoff had a weakness and that was his love for the ladies. He could never be true to just one at a time, but it caught up with him one night and it was a night that would never be forgotten. Geoff was married to his children's mother, but was having an affair with another woman after he and his wife Danica began having problems. He used their constant arguments as an excuse to step out on his wife of 12 years. One day while getting Geoff's clothes together to be dry-cleaned, Danica came across a number in his shirt pocket with a woman's name on it. This pissed Danica off to the point of seeing blood. "I'm tired of this Don Juan wannabe sucker thinking that he is going to handle me, but I got something for his ass." Putting her plan into motion, she cooked Geoff's favorite meal that day as she wondered what would be the best way to let his cheating ass know that she was on to him. She took the kids to her mom's house and went home to wait on her husband. This was not the first time that she had found numbers in his pockets, hell she had even found condoms in his car, but she was just fed the fuck up by now with his disrespectfulness. Geoff came home that evening around 8:00 2 hours late for dinner as usual.

"Where are the kids"?

"They're at my mom's house, I thought that you and I could have some alone time.

"Sure baby, we haven't had that in a long time.

"What's for dinner?"

"I fixed steak with onion gravy, new potatoes, snow peas and some peach cobbler."

"Damn baby, you fixed it up for papa didn't you girl?"

"Nothing is too good for my man."

"I ran a hot bath for you so that you can get comfortable before you eat."
"That's what I'm talking about right there, take care of your man girl."

Danica went about her business in the kitchen checking on a big pot that she had on the stove. She gave Geoff ten minutes head start so that he could get comfortable in the tub. She turned the stove off and removed the pot and went to peek her head in the door to see if Geoff needed anything while he relaxed. She took him a cold beer wrapped in paper at the bottom. The curtain was closed and it brought memories of happier times for them. She was almost tempted to join him in the tub, but the thought quickly left her mind when she thought about the phone number she had found earlier in his pants. She sat the beer beside the tub and made another trip into the kitchen to get one more thing.

"Geoff, I brought you a beer," she said as she pulled the curtain open and handed the beer to her husband.

"Girl, you know I'm a ma .A man don't need no napkin around his cold brew because we swallow our shit in one gulp." She took the paper off for him, but it fell in the tub right in his chest. "Let me get this for you before it gets wet, you may need this number and, Danica pretended to be reading the name but she knew the name all too well.

"You may need to call Tracy", Geoff got choked as he was swallowing his beer."

"Let me get you a drink of water for that cough." Danica then snatched the curtain back and produced the big pot that she had on the stove and doused Geoff's body with boiling water mixed with baby oil.

"Ah shit, what the fuck is wrong with you bitch?" The water had hit him in the chest and down his stomach and seemed to be sticking with the oil mixed in with it.

"I'm going to kill you bitch as soon as I get the fuck out of this tub!!" Got damn this shit is burning."

Danica stepped out of his reach and waited for him to get out of the tub. His body was slippery from the baby oil, so when he got out, he fell to the floor while reaching for Danica. She wasn't finished yet, when he fell face forward on the floor, she got the other pot she had waiting for him and doused his back. This one was so hot that his skin immediately started peeling off of his back. Geoff could only cuss and roll his body around on the floor, which only made the burns worse. Danica saw the damage that she had done and ran out of the house. She dialed a number praying that the person would pick up. "Hello, sister dear, how are you this evening?"

Without hesitation, Danica blurted out, "Your brother need some medical attention right away, he is hurt very badly."

Katrina took the phone away from her ear, looking at it as if she could see Danica's face. "Where is he now?"

"Laying on the bathroom floor of our house and Katrina, I'd hurry if I were you." Click. Katrina and Deborah had made it there in less than forty minutes and when they found their brother passed out on the floor with pinkish grey skin showing on over half of his body, they just knew he was dead. Geoff had passed out from the shock and pain. He awakened at the sound of Deborah calling his name and asking if Danica did this to him. "Yeah, that bitch has lost her damn mind." Geoff said through agonizing pain.

"Nah, she hasn't lost it yet, but she will as soon as I get to her." Katrina stated as her eyes glistened with tears at seeing her brother's body burned.

"This bitch has the game fucked up if she thinks that her ass is getting off for this", Katrina stated.

With all the pain that Geoff was in, he still realized how protective his sisters were and pleaded with them to let him handle it. "I think you have handled enough if you ask me," came a voice from behind them. Deborah took one leap and had Danica down on the floor beating her with everything she had inside of her. Geoff was yelling for Katrina to get Deborah off of Danica, but she was busy getting one of the jars of still burning candles that Danica had for the fake romantic setting. Katrina separated the two women and asked Deborah to please call the paramedics. Geoff witnessed his sisters wrath and protectiveness as one called for help while the other one took a jar of hot wax poured it over his wife's face and then stomped her bloody while he had looked on in horror

Geoffrey Grey had become a very wealthy young man with a keen business sense coupled with his street knowledge. Andreas had brought him into his world and it had proven to be beneficial to both parties. As Geoff was getting ready to leave from work on this day, his phone rang and his secretary informed him who was calling, a scowl came over his face as he told her to send the call through. "Yes Kyle, all I need to know from you is have you taken care of that business for me?"

"Geoff, I just wanted to personally let you know that the assignment has been completed."

"Alright, I'll be in touch," he stated as he hung up the phone. Geoff was ready to end the workday and have a relaxing evening with one of his many female companions. But that thought was cut short when he received a call from Katrina asking him to join the family at their parent's home. Geoff always became nervous whenever he received a phone call from his family, because of his eldest sister's illness. The siblings were well into adulthood and had gained their own families and problems, but the Grey family still remained as one. The meeting ground was always at their parent's modest home.

GREY FAMILY DINNERTIME

Deborah Grey-Simms had three children by now, Bryson, Braxton and Bridgette. Geoffrey had three children that lived in Atlanta, but the family rarely saw his children after he and Danica's divorce. Katrina had one son, Damien Junior better known as Flex. Bryson and Braxton were only two years apart and practically inseparable, but once Flex turned sixteen, Bryson allowed him to hang out with them a little from time to time. The boys had gotten involved in a money making scheme that they were making sure their parents didn't find out about. Bryson aka G and Braxton aka Tyga were into dog breeding. The family was dog friendly and the boys had taken a liking to Pitt Bulls.

They started out with breeding and selling them until Flex presented the idea to them about raising a more fierce species of bulldog for dog fighting and how much more money they could potentially make. Flex told them about injecting the dogs with heroin to make them more aggressive. G's first question to Flex was how in the hell did he know about heroin. Flex explained to them how he learned in his chemistry class about the drug being used in labs on animals and how it would make them more aggressive. They knew that Flex was a physics freak and didn't doubt his word after hearing him explain in detail how it works.

They began injecting heroin into the puppies in small doses and soon became the most popular Pitt Bull breeders in the area. It became known that if you wanted a badass dog, just contact the Grey boys and you couldn't go wrong. They would bet on the dogs that they knew were bought from them and the money was pouring in by the boatload. The boys would soon find out that the illegal money is the most addictive and dangerous money you could make. When the boys got to their grandparents home, Katrina was there as was Bridgette and her children. They went into Deborah's bedroom to talk to her and see how her day was going. Deborah had moved back in with her parents once she was diagnosed with her illness.

"Hey mama, how are you feeling today?" G asked his mom as he leaned down to hug her.

"I'm doing alright," she answered with a weak smile as Tyga was now hugging her and then Flex took his turn. The boys always flocked to give their mom and Auntie love and comfort, as they knew she was getting more ill, but she never once complained of the pain that her body was enduring. They were asking if she needed anything to eat or drink and it just warmed Deborah's heart to know that her family loved and adored not only each other so much, but how everyone catered to her every need and want. She loved the attention that she got from her boys. They were mama's boys and everyone knew it. She always spoiled them to no end, but she gave her daughter Bridgette tough love. Katrina and Mama Joe always told her over the years that she should give more attention to Bridgette instead of the boys, but she always stood firm that Bridgette got all the attention that she needed from her. Katrina and Mama Joe made up for the attention that they felt Bridgette didn't get from her mother. Bridgette and Katrina were very close and Bridgette was more like Katrina than any of them knew, but in time Katrina would find out just how alike they really were.

The boys went into the kitchen to see what Mama Joe had cooked and to their delight, there was a feast laid out. Mama Joe was sitting in the dining room with her great grandbabies as they played and ran around. G's babies' mamas had brought them over earlier in the day and Tyga's little girl along with Bridgette's little girl Chyna was all about to drive Mama Joe crazy. They would all joke around with Deb about her having the worst grandkids they had ever seen, but they all spoiled them nonetheless.

G, Tyga, Flex and Twan decided to indulge in a game of NBA 2K13 until the family was ready to eat. Twan, the honorary youngest Grey sibling never got to follow the older boys, but when they were there, he felt proud to be a part of the crew. He looked forward to the day that he could follow them on one of their excursions.

"Y'all boys have been gone all day and you just walk in here and start playing on my damn T.V without speaking to your Grandma," Granny Joe fussed. G was the first to get over to her and hugged her neck while giving her a peck on the cheek. "You know I love my favorite ole girl," laughed G. Flex as usual had to get a rise out of his Grandma. "Hey Granny Joe, this is our room, why are you in here?"

"This is my got damn house and I go into any room I want to go into in this joint. You ain't paying not one damn bill in here and you better shut the hell up before I put your ass out of my house." The boys all knew that Granny Joe would never actually put them out of her house, in fact if they skipped a day coming over, there was hell to pay for not showing their faces.

She got her joy out of talking smack to her grandkids and kids, but if someone else ever dared to do talk like this to any of them, her joking around became someone's worst nightmare. The jokes went out the window where her babies were concerned.

"Granny Joe you can't put me out of here, Pops pay the bills in here."

"Pops pay the bills, but I am the boss." Flex and Tyga usually liked to get their Grandmother riled up like this because at times she could out curse a drunken sailor and it would always make the boys laugh to watch her feistiness come out. She enjoyed the chance to joke around with her Grand-boys as well. Katrina walked into the room and told Flex and Tyga to leave their Grandmother alone.

"Auntie I ain't said nothing, that was Flex," Tyga said in his usual country drawl." Yes I know baby boy, you never aggravate your grandmother now do you? "Mama, have you talked to Geoffrey yet?" Katrina was talking to her nephew and mom all while setting the dinner table.

"Yes I have and he should be coming through the door at any minute now." Just as the words left Granny Joe's mouth, Geoff walked in the room looking flyy as always dressed from head to toe in Armani.

"It's about time your whorish ass got here, your sister here is worrying me to death asking when you would get here,"

"Mama, I only just asked if you've heard from Geoffrey. Could you stop being so dramatic woman?" Katrina kidded with her mom.

"I'm going to get Deb so that we can all eat," Katrina said as she left the room to get her sister. "Debby are you ready to eat?" Katrina was the only one in the family that had taken to calling her sister Debby.

"What kind of question is that to ask?" Deb asked as she chuckled. Since the illness, her appetite had doubled and she always made demands about what she would like to eat. She had developed diabetes and it had become quite severe, most times getting to dangerously high and randomly getting dangerously low. She had a rare condition, which affected the hormones, liver and/or pancreas. Her illness just so happened to have affected both her liver and pancreas. Since the pancreas controls the sugar level in the human body, her blood sugar had no way of staying stable without constant monitoring and insulin injections. Because of this, the family had to try to control what she ate. This was no easy feat to do because the sweet natured Deb had become somewhat mean as hell, but she was loved nonetheless. Katrina assisted Deb into the dining room to take a seat at her favorite spot. Deborah looked at all of the food on the table which consisted of baked chicken and fried chicken for those that didn't want baked, string beans with red new potatoes, steamed cabbage, candied yams and hot water corn bread. Mama Joe always went above and beyond for her family when she knew the whole gang would be on deck to eat.

Deborah took in all that was on the table and told Katrina that she would take a little of everything. "I don't think so sister dear," Katrina said as she began fixing Deb's plate of food with what she knew would be safe for her sister to eat. "I'm so tired of you treating me like I am a child." Deborah said with a frown on her face. Katrina just continued to fix her sister a plate and pretended not to hear her. Deborah knew she was fighting a losing battle with Katrina, but just had to give it a try. She also knew that once everyone had left, that Mama Joe would give her what she wanted or she would just simply go into the kitchen and get what her appetite desired. Katrina was forever telling Mama Joe to cook only what Deborah was allowed to eat and that the rest of the family would adjust to a more healthy eating habit.

Mama Joe being the old-school cook that she was just refused to make healthy meals. The Grey family enjoyed their moments like these that they were having at this moment. Katrina looked at her family and just smiled as she silently prayed for each of them to have inner strength. She knew her sister did not have long to be with them and prayed that God would give her family the strength they needed to get through their hard times. No one wanted to talk about the situation with Deborah, but Katrina knew it was unavoidable. Katrina began fixing the plates with the help of Bridgette and eased in the conversation that she'd had with Deborah's Doctor. "Dr. Atkinson has reported that Deborah's illness is not responding to the treatment as well as it did when they first began treating her." Deborah began to get an irritated expression on her face.

"Why are we having this discussion without my husband's presence?"

"He was called and invited, but we are all hungry and you needed to get something to eat before your evening meds, I'm sure he will be here shortly." stated Katrina. Now Katrina wore the irritated look of disgust on her face. It was no secret of the bitterness she held for her brother-in-law.

"Well he's not stopping y'all from eating, but I will not discuss anything without Trevor's presence. Regardless of how any of you feel about him, he is still my husband and I refuse to exclude him of any discussions when concerning me". Katrina continued to fill her dad's plate as all eyes were on her and Deb at this point. G eyes began to bulk, Flex rolled his eyes up to the ceiling, Tyga was only concerned with eating and Bridgette was secretly steaming on the inside. She knew exactly why her dad was not yet there and understood how her Aunt felt. Katrina fixed her own plate and took a seat next to her son as she began to eat. Without looking up from her plate, Katrina continued to inform the family members beginning with her mom and ending with her Niece and Nephews about the options for her sister. "She can continue to take the chemo in pill form and it may or may not prolong her life, but she will have a quality life. She can continue to take the more powerful Chemo and run the risk of getting weak sooner than later. "At this point we can only do what is most comfortable for her."

Deborah coughed and said, "Kat don't be speaking about me as if I am not even here and this is a decision that Trevor and I should be making, not my family." No one dared to tell Deb that Trevor had started living his life as if she didn't exist. Her family could not bring that type of burden on her with everything going on in her life. How could they tell her that word had gotten back to them that Trevor was seen with his mistress having dinner?

"Deborah I completely understand what you are saying, but I guess Trevor had to work late and could not make it this evening," Mama Joe then spoke up saying, "You know that we will let him know everything concerning your health even if he cannot find the time to be here for you." Granny Joe was becoming upset and allowing her emotions to guide her instead of a rational head and her statement caused a roomful of eyes to cast her way. No one had the nerves to call her on it except Katrina and that's what she did in a very subtle way. "Mama, I tried to turn that oven off, but could not get it to go off. Could you come and take a look at it for me?" Katrina said as she gave her mom the evil eye.

Just as mother and daughter were getting up to excuse themselves from the table, the doorbell rang. Thomas got up to answer the door while the ladies went into the kitchen. Granny Joe also wanted to see who was at the family door during supper. As she was walking into the kitchen, she came face to face with Trevor. "It's about time you made a damn appearance, your wife has been waiting for you." Thomas waved his wife's comment off and welcomed Trevor in. "Don't pay this damn woman no mind, come on in here son and get a plate of this good food prepared by that evil lady," Thomas chuckled referring to his wife. They all returned back to the dinner table, but not before Mama Joe gave her husband a dirty look that spoke volumes. Katrina asked her mom if she would be a little more conscious of what she said to and around Deborah and how she said it. Like always, mama didn't take kindly to anyone telling her how to act and simply stated, "Hell she knows he isn't worth a shit. Speaking of isn't worth a shit, where is your so-called husband this evening? Oh yeah, I forget that we are not good enough for him to eat with us," Mama continued to rant.

"Mama, Damien is out of town on business this week," "I should have known that is what you were going to tell me. Hell every week he is out of town. He may have you fooled child, but I am not fooled by a long shot. While you we have word on Trevor taking his mistress out in the public eye, I guess your husband is at least smart enough to have his fling out of town."

Katrina just shook her head because she knew that her mother was going to think what she wanted to think no matter what anyone said, so why bother. It's not like she could tell any of them the real reason he was always out of town. Katrina and her mother joined the family back at the table and Trevor had taken a seat next to Deborah holding her hand. Katrina looked towards Trevor and brought him up to date with what they were discussing. Katrina detested Trevor since finding out about his affair with this skank of a bitch while her sister was battling this incurable illness. If he thought for one second that he was getting away with that shit, he had a call waiting on him. The only reason that she had not approached him as of yet is because she didn't want to bring any more worry on her sister. "*In due time Trevor Dent, in due time*" thought Katrina. Trevor smiled and only said, "whatever the family thought would be best for his wife that he was in agreement." The decision to continue treatment would ultimately be Deborah's, choice, but she valued the opinion of her family and trusted them whole heartily. They were all silently praying for a miracle to come into their family as they sat for the evening family dinner.

G, TYGA & FLEX

It was now late October and Flex, along with his cousins G and, Tyga were at Flex's home awaiting a phone call. G's phone began to vibrate in his pocket and he got up to step outside to take the call because the boys were in Damien's game room and had the music loud with a game of pool already in full effects.

"You get that business taken care of yet? The voice on the other end asked.

"Handled with no problem as always and I expect my paper to be proper just the same with no cuts. Meet me at the spot in one hour and I can get you and your boys straight. Have I ever had a problem with the paper before concerning my number one partnas?"

"Nah and nothing personal, but as you said this is business. See you in one hour."

G returned to the game room to let the boys know they needed to get back to business. "That was money calling fellas, let's go get this chedda," There was an old house across town run by a dude named Frank, he always have illegal activities of every sort going on and he cashed in with a profit from everyone that came through his door. As they drove through town they saw the town's people admiring the Halloween scenery that was spread throughout the small downtown area. They passed by pumpkin sceneries, scarecrow sceneries and even zombies with human like faces. Man this shit is creepy late at night," thought Flex.

The boys pulled up to Frank's house that looked as if the county should condemn it and shut the engine off. "Man all of this money Frank has coming through here, why in the hell doesn't he get him a decent place to live," Flex stated.

"That ain't how the game goes lil' cuz. This man has to keep a low profile and stay off the radar. He can't do that if he up and get a nice crib with no legitimate job," G schooled Flex. Just as they stepped out of the car they heard footsteps approaching them. All three boys went for their burners until Flex realized that he didn't have a damn thing on him. "G is going to have to get over me carrying some heat," thought Flex.

Boobie the neighborhood crack head was out trying to scratch up some money for a hit. "I'll wash this car for you man for five dollars."

"Damn Boobie you got to stop sneaking up on folks for five fucking dollars and how the hell you gone wash my car this time of night?" Take this ten and get the hell away from me Boobie, I'm busy right now man. But this should get you through for a minute," G stated as he knocked on the door in a code, which caused Tyga to laugh like hell.

"Why don't you just huff and puff and blow this raggedy bitch down since it's only held together by a splinter anyway"? This caused Flex to bend over with laughter as well and even G had to chuckle at that one. The door was just barely hanging on by the hinges, but he honored his friend Franks request and did the signature knock each and every time. Frank came to the door looking up and down the road on some ole double 07 shit and this only caused the three to laugh even harder.

"What the hell so got damn funny? Bring y'all asses on in before somebody roll up in here."

By this time Tyga, the comedian of the three was rolling on the floor laughing as Frank dead bolted the door and they could still see the outside traffic through the holes. "Frank, you on some other shit dude. Give us our damn money for disposing of those wounded dogs for your ass so we can be out," said Tyga with tears in his eyes from laughing so hard.

"How much I owe y'all dudes and don't be tryna take the damn head price up either." Frank was a comical dude and kept you laughing even without trying to be funny.

"You owe us nine thousand, six hundred for eight heads, that's twelve hundred a head," Flex stated.

"What, I had eight of them muther-fuckers to die on me? Shit I bought them from y'all grimy ass, I shouldn't pay shit."

Tyga quickly stopped all laughter at this point and became very serious. "Look here bitch nicca, you get the pups and it's up to you to train them to be fighters or be a bitch like you. Do you inject them properly? Because it sound to me, you are doing something wrong, now pay us the damn money you owe and we can be on our way," G tried to take control of the situation before it got out of hand, his brother could have a temper at times and when his money was in question he could get dangerous.

"Tyga, come on man, you know Frank is just having fun don't get so bent out of shape all the time."

"Naw B, if his punk ass wasn't so paranoid, he could come out and see what the hell his dogs be doing to get their ass kicked all the time, but he hiding out like fucking George In The Jungle and don't know what the hell be going on."

By now Frank was coming back out of the room with a fistful of bills in his nervous hands. "Count that shit out man!" yelled Tyga. "You don't come bringing no shit balled up like you in a candy store? What the hell kind of business is that?"

After collecting their money and a promise from Frank of doing better business next time the boys left. Flex tallied up their money from the many dogfights and breeding. The boys were sitting on top of 300 stacks apiece. G told Flex it was time for him to exit the game and take his earnings to pay for his school of choice. Flex thought it was time as well and as soon as school started back, he planned on making the whole family proud of him. G and Tyga both had plans to move to more legit ways of living as well. G had three children and Tyga had two, they all just wanted better for their families. Flex had his sights set on going to Tuskegee, while G and Tyga had plans of opening a top of the line car dealership. Although they had very little money for the big plans they had, they did have the most powerful tool needed for their success without the knowledge of them even realizing that tool.

The trio headed back to the Grey's family home and with a renewed feeling of peace they decided to take the route through town to sight see all of the Halloween displays the small town had to offer. They parked their car and decided to walk and enjoy the displays like the many other people that were admiring the Halloween decorations. It reminded them of the movies Friday The 13th and A Nightmare On Elm Street. They had even seen a Jason and Freddie Kruger scarecrow when they rode through earlier. Walking through town was so refreshing after making up their minds to leave the hood life behind. Being green to the game neither young man realized that once you chose the hood life, the only way out is jail or hell. The town's people were out and plentiful this cool October night just strolling checking out the Halloween scenes, the children were holding tight to their parent's hands as they stopped by the displays of spooky themes. G was feeling generous and decided to go by the local grocer and get assorted candy to put at each display. Flex and Tyga said they would just hang out till he returned. On the short drive there, G listened to an up and coming Rich Homie Quan. The song was titled INVESTMENTS and it was right on point after the conversation he and the boys just had:

I got a bank like an investor, I'm a CEO the game
And they hate cuz I'm successful for myself I made a name
Niggas said that they would help you but they really all the same
And I finally realized that
These Niggas just want to see me down,
Want to see me fall
Want to see me down and fucked up
Hope to god I'm dead and locked up
Niggas just want to see me down,
Want to see me fall
Want to see me down and fucked up
Praying to God I'm dead and locked up

G was so busy bopping his head to the beat of Rich Homie Quan, that he didn't notice the black on black Escalade trailing behind him. He came to a traffic light and leaned down to retrieve his ringing cell phone that had fell to the floor. The Escalade pulled beside him and he never noticed the chrome barrel sticking out of the back passenger window. Rounds of shots seemed to endlessly fire into the body of G's car and the Escalade made a left at the light with the belief that G was dead.

Tyga and Flex heard the shots, as did all the other town's people because they were only a block away. Flex looked at Tyga who was beside the Freddie Kruger life like scarecrow and said. "Man what the hell was that?" Tyga started to say let's go check it out, but before he

45

could get his words out the scarecrow that was holding a sword like knife stepped out and started wielding the sharp knife in the direction of the boys. Flex saw the scarecrow move and knocked Tyga to the ground just in time, but not before the sword caught him behind his right thigh. People were screaming and running wild by now and local authorities that were nearby, sprang into action and gave chase to the scarecrow as he dashed behind abandoned buildings and through alleyways. Camouflaged as a scarecrow was a dude named Rick, and he was there to avenge the death of his brother Reece. Rick lost the policemen and on a back road the Escalade was waiting for him. Meanwhile ambulances were at the scene of the shooting and upon arrival they were in awe of the bullet holes in the car and knew that the poor passengers could not have survived the attack.

Tyga was in a panic at this time. His little cousin was lying on the ground bleeding after saving him from the same fate and G was taking forever to get back. "Flex, hang in there man. Here comes the cops now, shit we don't need this right now. Man, are you hurt badly? Damn I can't stand all of this blood man!!!" Tyga was pacing around Flex and he lay out on the concrete trying to keep calm. He knew that Tyga hated the sight of blood, but hated the cops even more, so he knew that at any moment his big cuz was going to lose it.

"Tyga, I'm fine man, just help me up to a sitting position before they get over here." The officers approached the two and went for their guns right away, assuming that Tyga was the attacker after seeing him

46

bending over Flex."

"Freeze, put your hands up where we can see them sir." Tyga dropped Flex right where he was causing a burning sensation to radiate down the injured leg. "Son, what happened here?"

"Officers, this is my cousin Braxton Dent and he was trying to help me up after I was attacked."

"Are you Trevor Dent's son sir?"

"Yes he is."

"Deborah is your mother and Katrina is your Aunt?

"Yes to both of those questions and this is my cousins Flex. Katrina is his mom."

The two officers suddenly had a change in their demeanor. "Son do you need some medical attention?" Officer Scott asked of Flex.

"No sir, if I can just get to my grandmother's house, my mom is there and can take care of me."

Officer Scott was on Damien and Katrina's payroll and knew that Katrina would want to take care of this situation herself. "Any idea of who did this to you?"

"On one, we were only sightseeing with the rest of the people here and I tripped and fell landing on something sharp when I heard some gunshots."

"You boys be careful, there was a car that got shot up at the traffic light just a block away." They both became nervous when the cop pointed in the direction in which G had driven. People were still surrounding Flex asking if he was okay. They were only being concerned, but they were really getting on his nerves invading his space like that. Just as Tyga was about to dial G's number, he heard someone yelling his name. He looked up and to his relief, he saw G making his way through the crowd.

G drove as fast as possible to where Tyga and Flex was and began to panic upon seeing Tyga standing over a bleeding Flex. "Awe man, what the fuck happened to my lil' cousin?" G asked as he pushed his way through the crowd that had begun to surround Flex. He began yelling Tyga's name to get his attention and noticed the look of relief that crossed over Tyga's face.

"What happened here?" Tyga gave a brief on what happened to them and G gave a brief on what he had witnessed back at the traffic light. "I don't know what the hell is going on, but I know that those bullets were meant for me and then someone tried to get at y'all." Luckily for G, he had heard the first shot and had ran the red light, but the car behind him was not so lucky as it was the car that had received all of the shots except one.

"We got to get Flex to the hospital, he's losing blood. "No, take me to Granny Joe's house to my mama. She'll know what to do."

"Man you crazy, you bleeding like a wounded hog and you think we're going to Granny Joe's house?" G looked at Flex like he was really on the short bus, because everyone knew that Katrina was going to flip out when she laid eyes on a bloody Flex.

"It's just a flesh wound", said Flex and he was right. Even though he had blood everywhere, thankfully it was only a flesh wound and because his mom was a nurse and never took little scrapes seriously he knew that he was fine. They got into the car driving with haste to their Grandparent's house. "G what was all of that shooting we heard coming from where you were?"

" Oh yea, this black Escalade pulled up beside me while I was fiddling around the floor board looking for my phone. I lifted my head up and saw a damn nine pointed right at me. I stomped the gas to the floor, but they still shot the back fender. Flex was in the back seat with bulging eyes, but not from the pain of getting cut, he feared the wrath that he knew his mom was going to give him. " I've got to get my shit together for real now." thought Flex.

The boys were playing a dangerous game that they had no idea how to play due to the fact that, although they were in the hood a lot visiting their homies, they were never allowed to hang out with those same boys as they were growing up. So it was like they were green to the real game. Flex being the youngest of the boys and his mother's only child was shielded more so than his older cousins. All three were what one would call pretty boys, but with a harsh lifestyle and numerous baby mommas, G was shedding out of his pretty boy looks and getting a more matured thug appearance and even wore a gold grill when he was not around his family. He could still turn the heads of many females even though he never thought of himself as an eye catcher. G was about 5'9 and 145 pounds with smooth skin the color of honey. He had dark brown eyes and one lone dimple in his right cheek that drove the women crazy when he smiled. He kept his hair in medium dreads that came just to his shoulders. G had two baby mamas, but was not currently with either. This didn't, however stop him from being a great dad. If anything it only made him want to be present more in his children's lives. Before his mom's illness, she would keep his kids and her other grandkids every weekend. His Mom, Grandma, sister and especially his Aunt didn't particularly care for the mother of two of his children and the only thing that kept Katrina off of her after she pulled some shady charges against G, was the love for her Great Nephew and Niece.

Tyga had only one baby mama name Keisha. They were living together raising their daughter Bevy and Keisha's two older sons with a little one on the way. Tyga stood about 5'9 tall as well and weighted about the same at 145 pounds. Although he and G were two years apart and had different fathers, they could almost go for twins. Tyga had skin of golden honey like his older brother G and he actually had long dreads that hung down to the middle of his back that Keisha kept looking flyy as hell. Tyga could turn heads of the young and old, but he knew Keisha would kick his ass if he even acted like he was looking in the direction of another woman. He truly loved his woman so he never even wanted to stray and his motto was *"if a woman is giving me all that I want, why do I need to get out and look for something else."*

Flex was only 17 with honey golden skin and those sexy light brown eyes that he inherited from his mother seemed to get brighter in the light and drove the women crazy. The opposite sex young and old would always flirt to no end with him often making Katrina give the older ones the evil eye. Flex was small in stature however, often being mistaken for a 12 year old, but his mom & dad refused to let that be a hindrance to him. He was taught at an early age that if he came home with a whooped ass due to not defending himself, then he was going to get an even worse whooped ass for not standing his ground. His size and looks often fooled his peers into thinking that he was easy prey for bullying, but his first year in middle school proved that theory wrong.

The year was 2007 and Flex had gotten accepted into the local prestigious Fine Arts Academy for his upcoming 6th grade year. This

was all his mom's idea, sure he passed all the exams to get in because he
knew had he failed, she would have torn him a new asshole. Flex was
proud that he made it in and his parents were just as elated, but he started
to notice that this scene was not for him. There were rainbows all over
the school and his mom noticed as well. 'Flex if I ever catch you with
your wrist flipped, I'll break it clean in two and she meant every word.
Then she would punch him in his chest as if she was caving it in and tell
him to man the hell up and be about his books, but if anyone got out of
pocket with him, he better damn well put them back in their place. Well
one day, sure enough, an 8th grader was conspicuously making a pass at
Flex and next thing you know the principle was calling his mom in about
his atrocious behavior. "What's the problem Ms. Davis?"

"The problem Mrs. Cunningham is that Flex has attacked one the
students this morning breaking the student's nose and jaw in the
process."

The women seemed to be five types of nervous as she wrung her
hands while trying to appear to be in control. "This type of behavior is
not acceptable in this school. Flex's mom Katrina asked to speak with
her son alone.

"Mama let me explain something first," she grabbed him by the
collar and told him it better be damn good to get her out of the office in
the middle of working. He explained how the boy had made a pass at him
detail for detail and it took everything in Katrina not to go berserks
herself. Katrina had a temper, but she knew how to bring it out in a nice
nasty manner. "Go get your book bag and get in the car" she told him as

the Principle came back into the office. "Ms. Davis I am appalled by all of this that has happened today," Katrina was cut off by Ms. Davis, "I'm sure you will understand my position in suspending your son from our school."

"What the hell just happened? I know this woman is talking out the side of her neck," thought Katrina.

"No, you obviously do not understand Ms. Davis, an inappropriate gesture was made towards my son today and yes he handled it the wrong way, but he was protecting himself. Now I don't condone my son starting fights, but rest assured he is taught by his father and myself to protect himself if provoked. Now my son may be suspended, but best believe that the student that made a pass at my boy will have sexual harassment charges pressed against him and this school will be investigated for allowing these acts to take place. Because Ms. Davis I can count on one hand the number of male students that seem to be straight. You are not blind and I assume that you are not crazy. You see what is going on around this school just like any person that visits or work here sees.

Ms. Davis was sitting in her chair with an appalled look on her face and mouth slightly open at this point, but it did not seem to phase Katrina as she continued to express her displeasure with what had taken place. Katrina was about to come unglued and knew she had to get control over her emotions before she lost it on this dried up peace of trash in front of her. "You can close your mouth and stop pretending that you don't know what is going on around this school. As a matter of fact, I'll get with some of the other parents and have them to question their children to see

have any similar incidents happened with their kids and maybe they have
been too afraid to come fourth about it. You see Ms. Davis, I am aware
that 'this school' does not want real boys to attend, but with the intellect
my son has you have no other choice now do you?" With that being said,
Katrina walked out to the car and told her son a job well done. Hell she
wanted to find the little fucker herself and punish him for coming at her
son like he was a punk.

Present day in time Flex's leg had slowed up bleeding as he was
assisted into his Granny Joe's house with the help of his cousins through
the back door, but was spotted by Bridgett's 5-year-old daughter Chyna.
His pants leg was covered in blood and Chyna being the little pristine girl
that she is immediately started firing questions and screaming for her
Auntie to come into the kitchen.

"What happened to you Flex?" You are dirty and stinky looking.
Why do Uncle G and Uncle Tyga have to help you walk?" Tee Tee, Flex
is hurt badly, come in here hurry up!! She had said all of this in one
breath and without breaking a sweat. Katrina walked in and upon seeing
Flex's blood soaked pants she got weak in the knees. She was use to
handling emergencies on her job and had seen much worse, but when it
came to her family, it was a different story. Katrina regained her
composure after Flex spoke up, "Ma I'm fine, and it's only a flesh
wound,"

"Flesh wound my ass!" said Katrina as she ripped the pants from
around his leg to inspect it. By now the whole family was in the room

54

and Granny Joe started demanding answers as Bridgette assisted her Aunt in checking Flex's wound. "What do you think Bridgette?" Katrina asked of her niece. Bridgette was currently in her second year of intern to receive her degree in medicine. She still was in limbo as to what she would specialize in, but was leaning towards Pediatrics. Katrina was an RN by trade, but she and her childhood friend Monica had decided to explore the Chiropractic field. They now owned their own practice and employed new graduates of Chiropractic and sport medicine programs. She was secretly hoping that Bridgette would choose sports medicine, but was just happy that her niece had chosen the medical field. This would prove to be beneficial for the family in the future. Bridgette grabbed her medical bag and went to work on Flex and was happy to report that just as they suspected, the sword had narrowly missed slicing the artery in the back of his thigh. Flex only had to have about ten stitches because the wound was mostly superficial. Just as rehearsed the boys gave the false version of what actually happened. 'They were walking in the downtown area sight-seeing the Halloween displays and horse playing when Flex fell backwards and onto a display with a scare crow holding a sword. Of course Katrina didn't buy this, but knew eventually the truth would come out. Later that night while Flex & Katrina were watching a movie, something they often did when Damien was out of town on business, Flex was wondering why did he try to fit in at this new school so hard. The family had just recently moved back to their hometown and Flex wanted to fit in so badly that he became a totally different person. The old Flex would have never thought about fighting dogs, but the new Flex thought that it was intriguing to do something that the local guys deemed as cool.

KYLE

Back in Augusta Kyle was in deep thought, as he couldn't believe that he had almost ended the life of his best friend of 11 years. Flex and Kyle had become friends at their grade school in kindergarten and although they went to separate schools beginning their middle school years, the two had remained loyal to the friendship making sure to spend each other's birthday together. Katrina was like a second mom to Kyle and Flex was for sure his brother with another mother. "How did Flex get involved in this beef he wondered because he knew how both of Flex's parents were about him. I have to connect with him and find out what's going on.

Flex's cell phone alerted him of a text and when he checked it out he was excited to see his boy Kyle's number displayed with the simple word 'sup."

"My man what's up with you, haven't heard from you since I moved out to the boon docks"? Kyle responded with. "Hit me up tomorrow or better yet ask mom if I can come hang out with y'all for the weekend". Flex looked up at his mom who seemed to be engrossed in the movie, but was actually checking her son's reaction to the text. Since moving back home shed noticed after the break up with his girlfriend he didn't keep in touch with any of his friends from Augusta. "Mama, Kyle wants to know if he can come down this weekend and hang with me?"

"Of course he can, I'll handle your father on this one." Flex's dad

Damien never really approved of the friendship that his son had with Kyle and for that reason alone the boys had lost touch with each other except for getting together on the birthdays. "Tell him it's about time he looked in on his big brother." Katrina said with a chuckle. Although Flex was now a little shorter than Kyle, Flex was a few months older than Kyle and they always joked that Flex was the big Brother. Katrina really liked Kyle and considered him to be a second son and treated him as such even when the boys were in grade school together and she would often visit the school. If either boy got out of pocket in any way, Katrina would snatch a knot in their ass and they both knew this. The boys were older and knew that Mama Katrina would still tag the ass if need be with no problem which is why she didn't mind Kyle's visit.

The weekend arrived and Flex and Kyle were having the time of their lives. Damien had built his family a modest home that sat on 25 acres of land which was a dream come true for any male that loved sports and the great outdoors. During Kyle's visit, the boys kept busy despite being in the small town with no attractions, they spent the first day of his visit fishing in the 2 acre pond on the Cunningham's small estate, and of course played endless games of testosterone filled Madden. Their nights were filled with just riding around the small town and hanging around at the Greys', but there wasn't much to do to keep the local teens entertained. Flex began to fill Kyle in on what had been going on during his first summer as a true country boy. "Man you won't ever believe what I got myself into last week. Hell I don't believe it and I lived it."

58

Kyle twisted his lip and head in a doubtful manner and asked, "What the hell can you get into in this nothing ass town?"

"Yo, son I caught my first body last week then my older cousin was shot at while at the downtown traffic light while a damn scarecrow was a block away trying to kill my other cousin and me".

"Whoa, back the fuck up nicca. What do you mean you caught your first body?"

Flex reflected back to that night that changed his life forever. "Man let's ride out and have a little fun". Tyga stated. Flex's two cousins were considerably older than him and he was not allowed to hang out with them except going on errands for his mom, grand-mom or auntie. They all left with the pretense of getting some ice that was needed anyway since the entire family always had dinner together. This is something that they started doing almost a year ago when Deborah had been diagnosed with the illness. The three found themselves in a nearby neighborhood that was known for having constant criminal activities of all types. This was nothing for Tyga or G, but for Flex this was a new world and quite intriguing. This neighborhood also just happened to be famous for dog fighting and both G and Tyga were heavily involved with breeding Pitt bulls, but had been into dog fighting since Flex shared with them the money was nicer on the fighting side of the business. They were there to catch one of Tyga's prized Pitts, D-Block, go to battle. As Flex watched the fight, he was taken back to a time when he was only 8 years old and his mom was driving him to school. This particular morning they took the same route to Flex's elementary school that they took, but this morning they both saw a sight that would be etched in young Flex's mind all day that day. Some poor dog had gotten out of it's owners yard and had just been hit by a car just as Flex and Katrina were passing by. The poor thing was still breathing but was well into taking it's last breath, and this threw Flex into hysterics. He begged his mom to turn around to help the poor dog but Katrina, although hurt as well, knew there was nothing she could do. Flex decided that day to become a Veterinarian and vowed to always help animals from that day forward. It's funny how he had been lured into dog fighting now that he looked past back on that memory.

"I'll be able to nurse dogs back to health once I become a Veterinarian or be able to put them out of their misery. I guess the 'putting out of misery' part won't be as hard as I thought it would be when I was a child." The trill yelping of a dog brought him out of his daydream and back to the present. D-Block, the dog that Tyga sold some months ago had just viciously attacked another dog and the poor critter was barely breathing. This sight just tore Flex up to see the dog suffering so he took out his .22 and put him out of misery thus giving him his first murder. "You killed a damn dog? "Kyle was cracking up laughing at his friend Flex's version of catching a body.

"Nicca shut the fuck up and listen to the whole story." Anyway while we were all out there, this car kept driving by and we thought they were just checking out the dogs fighting. I had gone back to the car when next thing I know the car comes back and stops, three dudes step out looking for this dude named Reece. They said some cat had sent them to find him because of a debt he owed. The next day we were told the dudes had murked this Reece guy while he was down on his knees begging for his life. Flex never noticed the different stance Kyle had taken on once hearing Reece's name.

"So you weren't even there when the triggerman started busting shots?" asked Kyle.

"Hell to the naw. My ass had bent that corner before Dude hit the ground." Kyle was cracking up about his boy Flex's situation knowing that Ms. Katrina had a hard time cutting the umbilical cord and how hard his dad Damien was on him. How could he have ever thought that Flex could have ever been involved in something like this was crazy now that he thought about it, but was he really ready to give up his best friend of twelve years for the loyalty of his boss of four years? Well at least he didn't have to worry about Flex's life anymore now that he knew Flex wasn't involved. Unbeknownst to Flex, Kyle had become a different person than what he knew and if Katrina knew of what Kyle had become he would never step foot in her home again. Damien tolerated Kyle for his son and wife's sake, but picked up right away that something was amiss with the young man he never took a liking to after all of these years. Still Kyle wondered how Flex had even gotten involved with dog fighting.

"So um Flex, how did you come to get into dog fighting? I guess your cousins are teaching you all the ropes huh?"

"Naw man. I actually got them into it. A dude from my old neighborhood turned me on to it. When I found out about the money and how much you get when your mark wins, I just had to get in on making some of that money."

"Who is this dude?"

"His name is DJ". Replied Flex. Kyle had a look of bewilderment on his face, thinking to himself that this just could not be the same DJ he knew. But this would be something that this guy was into.

"So are you and DJ close friends?" Kyle asked Flex.

"Naw. We was just neighbors at one time back in Granite Hills." If this was the same DJ then Kyle had something to worry about concerning Flex because this DJ was next on his list to eliminate.

"Wait, I used to visit your house all the time there, and I never met a dude by that name before."

"D.J is much older than us. So you wouldn't remember him, but you remember his fine ass little sister Renee." She was the Puerto Rican chick that always gave us a peep show."

"I remember that honey, but I never knew she had a brother."

"Yeah, he was on lock down during that time, but he's the dude that turned me on to making this money and the partnership has been lovely". Flex stated while rubbing the palms of his hands together. Kyle became visibly shaken, because the DJ that he was assigned to murder was a Puerto Rican that was into the drug game pretty heavily.

"How does he fit into the Dog Fighting though man?"

"He told me how injecting the dogs with Heroin can make them more aggressive and man we haven't lost a fight since we started this method. It can vary from ten stacks up to fifty stacks on a single win and add the Breeding and selling that my cousins do and we are sitting pretty nice right about now."

Damn, this confirmed that they were indeed referring to the same guy and this put Kyle in a complicated position. If he didn't carry out his boss' orders then he knew orders would be carried out on him. Kyle knew he had to find out from Flex just how tight he and his cousins were connected to this DJ dude.

63

Flex took Kyle to meet the family he always told him about when they were younger and he shared funny stories with him about all of them. Everyone was there except his Uncle Geoffrey, but he knew his Uncle was always at the office and figured Kyle could meet him later. Kyle was introduced to the Grey family and, like everyone that met Granny Joe for the first time; he took an instant liking to Flex's grandmother. She was sharp with the tongue and knew everything about Kyle except his social security number in a matter of minutes. He could see where Ma Katrina got her feisty ways from as he was looking at the older version standing right before him. Kyle loved the family unity that Flex's family seemed to have, since his own family had just fallen apart. His mom and dad had been so in love, but for reasons unknown, they had recently divorced and this had taken an effect on Kyle and his family. He met the whole family and instantly felt a connection to the whole crew and he especially felt close to them now that he had met them and they made him feel like he was a member of the family. "Let's ride up to this girl's house that has been sweating me at school". Kyle decided to have a little fun with his man about Brandi. He knew Flex was not trying to leave Brandi for anyone. "Ooh how are you going to explain that to your girl in Augusta or have y'all broken up?"

"Naw man, we haven't broken up. That's my main girl and she isn't going nowhere." What she doesn't know won't hurt her. This chick is just a side piece I have a little fun with on the low."

Flex and Kyle had fun catching up with old times from the sandbox days. Kyle smiled slyly while looking over in Flex's direction and grinned. Flex knew that his boy was up to some slick shit right away and just waited for it to start dropping.

"Man I saw Keely at school and I swear to you the sun got brighter. That is a beautiful girl.

Flex sucked in his teeth and slightly shook his head in a knowing manner. "Why you got to bring her name up man?"

By now Kyle was nearly doubled over with laughter. Keely was Flex's first crush in Kindergarten. "Yo man, that will always be wifey number one dawg. We had the perfect wedding day picked out for you two love birds until someone ratted us out to your mom."

Both boys laughed at that memory. The entire second grade class at Warren Elementary had planned a wedding for Flex and Keely. They even had the honeymoon planned into the ceremony. Flex had complained to his mom that week about not wanting to get married.

"Boy you have years before you have to worry about getting married and by then you will want to." She'd said with a smile.

65

Upon Flex giving her details of this upcoming event being planned by these 8 year old kids, Katrina decided to make a trip to the school. Imagine her surprise when the entire school knew about it and thought it was cute. The mother of the bride was bringing cupcakes for the occasion. Katrina brought the devil back to life that day as she belittled each adult in her presence that day. Flex was both relieved and embarrassed knowing that this day would go down in history.

Shantega ran out of her house upon hearing the car horn. Flex texted to let her know he was coming through with a friend. Kyle eyed her body as she put an extra switch to her stride upon seeing that Flex had another guy with him. Kyle was thinking "Damn this pretty boy mutha fucker always get the baddest girls." That was until he saw the hair. "Damn, Flex doesn't usually go for the short nappy hair type but damn Shorty got some ass on her." He thought as he checked her out when she got to the car. I guess that's why Brandi is the main girl, but having a side piece like this to play with might be a little too much for my man to handle."

"What you getting into Shan with your fine self" asked Flex as he licked his lips.

"Nothing just bored is all with nothing to do," she said as she was trying to discreetly check out Kyle. "Who is your friend?"

"Oh yeah this is my homey Kyle. We have been thick since we had similac on our breaths back in grade school. Why don't you call a friend for him and we can all hang out together for a minute and go to my house for some fun. Tell her to bring a swim suite unless y'all prefer to go skinny dipping," Flex said while smiling.

"Are you out of your mind, it is too freaking cold to be going swimming Flex."

"Don't worry about all of that, just follow my instructions and do like I asked you to." Flex followed up like he was a real boss.

While Katrina was at her Mom's house and Damien Sr. was out of town, the four teens were at the Cunningham's place having a blast inside the pool house was well insulated. They decided to take a swim and cook some steaks on the grill. The party had gone into full blast when Katrina pulled up in her mint green 7 series Mercedes Damien had bought her as a bribe to move into the country land that she hated.

"What are you kids up to out here?"

"Hey Mama, I thought you would be at grandma's longer with Auntie."

"No I have company coming in this evening so Flex can you help me with these bags right quick?" Katrina asked.

"Just leave them in the car Ma, Kyle and I will get them in a minute!"

"FLEX!!! I asked YOU to help me get these bags out the car and I need YOU to do it now." Flex didn't miss a beat climbing out of the pool grabbing a towel to help his mother. After hearing her tone he knew his mom needed to speak with him about something privately. Flex grabbed the bags and followed his mom into the house. "Flex how long does your company plan on being here?"

"I'm not sure, but we won't get in your way, we'll just hang out in the pool house and listen to music."

"Well just so you know, Renee' is on her way down to visit and should be here in an hour."

"Okay that's fi"...... Flex stopped mid-sentence when it registered to him who his mother was talking about. "Renee? As in Brandi's mom?"

"Yeah but we won't get in you kids way." By the time Katrina had gotten that out of her mouth, Flex had raced back out into the pool house and raced to the swimming pool to break the party up and tell the girls to get dressed so he could take them home.

Kyle was like, "What the hell?" since he and Shan were really hitting it off. While the girls were in the pool house changing into their clothes, Flex told Kyle that Brandi's mom was on the way there and that he had to get Shan away from his house. Flex took Shan home and told her he would call her later on.

"So Kyle, what did you think of Shayla?" Little did Flex know Kyle was actually feeling Shan more than her friend Shayla, and Shan being the type of girl she is, was feeling him as well. The two had exchanged phone numbers while Flex was inside with his mother.

Eve, one of Katrina's best friends and partners with she and Monica had also come up to spend the weekend with her. Eve's husband Jason and Monica's husband Antonio were out of the country with Damien on business. "Eve, I am so glad you and the kids came to spend some much needed time with me. Brandi and her mom Renee' are on their way to spend the evening, but after they leave, I have a treat for the three of us."

"Will Monica be joining us as well?"

"Yes and you know we have not got our party on in quite a while girl."

"Oohh girl, tell me you got what I think you do."

"Straight from Jamaica boo." Katrina never let her guard down around anyone except for her girls, Monica and Eve and that's because she knew they would always have her back.

"I see a car coming in now, that must be Brandi and her Mom."

"Eve, I wish you could have seen the look on Flex's face when I told him that Renee` was coming to visit. His friend Kyle is here for the weekend and they had two girls out in the pool house with them. I did call him in the house to break the news to him and he broke a damn record getting them the hell away from here." laughed Katrina.

"I love this place girl," Renee' said as Katrina showed her around her new home. "Thank you so much." Renee' meet one of my best friends and business partners Eve Granger."

"Very nice to meet you Eve, any friend of Katrina's is a friend of mine."

"Nice to meet you as well and if you two would excuse me, I have to go and put baby down for a nap." Katrina and Renee' had become acquainted through their kids and had become quite cordial towards one another, but Katrina never viewed what they shared as a friendship and doubt they ever would. Katrina kept a close circle when it came to friends and other than Monica and Eve; she felt closeness to their office manager Sandy and head nurse Zaneta. Anyone else was out of the question. Brandi and Flex had attended the same affluent school before the Cunningham's moved to a smaller town.

"Yes girl I love it out here." The solitude it affords us is priceless." Eve was behind Renee making a face to show her dislike for the woman. Katrina was trying not to laugh so she averted her eyes from Eve and continued her conversation with Renee'." What Katrina wasn't telling is how much she detested living in such a small town and she hated the school system even more. However, Katrina did want to be closer to home after the diagnosis of Deborah so it was all worth leaving her city life. They had invested in a modest amount of land some years earlier so Damien decided to build the family a home there. "You know Renee', I really do miss the school there and I know that Flex misses Brandi a lot.

"Where is Brandi' by the way?"

"Girl she spotted your son as we were pulling up and jumped out of the car headed towards that pool house. I think it was smart to have a heated pool installed so Flex could have something to do year round. Lord knows he don't have much to do out here in these woods." Renee' stated as looked around with a taste of disdain on her face.

"Yes, that was Damien's idea. He really wanted to make it as comfortable for all of us, and fun at the same time. I'm just along for the ride," Katrina stated more sharply than she intended. "So Renee', how have you and Bill been doing?"

"We are great Katrina, but um, how you and Damien because I am picking up a little animosity from you about being here." Katrina looked up at Renee' from the bar where she was fixing them a glass of wine with somewhat of a smirk and thinking to herself, *"I know this heifer do not think that I will ever tell her my business for her to spread it around to everyone that will listen. She obviously does not know me and I sure as hell don't know you like that to share my personal space.* "No Renee', there is no animosity from me, in fact my husband made the right move at the right time and I couldn't be happier with my new home. Let's go out to the pool house with the kids and I can show you more of the great outdoors."

Hmm, let me find out that miss perfect Katrina and Damien are having problems. I don't know why she trying to pretend that they are the perfect couple and that nothing ever bothers her. She may as well decide to confide in me since we will be sharing a grandbaby soon. Renee' had

73

schooled Brandi' on how to get Flex and keep him the old fashioned way, but little did she know that Katrina had taught Flex just how to avoid little troubles like getting a baby and most of all how girls will try and trap a guy on purpose.

Katrina had witnessed how the people in her hometown operated and wanted Flex to be well aware to stay away from white girls because the small town frowned upon racially mixed dating. She told him to always protect himself whenever he had sex with a girl because most of them would entrap guys with a baby. She was always direct with her son and nephews and niece and they knew they could come to her about anything and not be judged. Flex was a little skeptical about opening up to his mother when it came to the sex talk, but he did listen to the advice she gave him. Katrina had no idea she had to worry about Flex having sex with Brandi' until she and Renee' walked into the pool house and saw the two teens completely nude and heavily engaged in a romp fest on the bed. Katrina's nose flared as her eyes turned completely grey with the sight she saw before her. Renee' on the other hand was all smiles as she thought, *"that's my girl, get that baby so we can be laid out in this mini castle."* Renee' saw the look on Katrina's face, but noticed that she was looking past the teens. She followed Katrina's stare and saw what had the lady more vexed than seeing her son in a love tryst with her daughter and let out a scream before fainting on the spot startling the couple out of their sex haze. "Momma," Flex yelled out as he and Brandi both struggled to cover themselves. He was trying to explain to his mom that it wasn't like she thought it was until he saw the look on his mother's face and the eyes of death that looked past him. He followed her stare and could not believe what his eyes were seeing and everything seemed to be going in slow motion as he watched the bullets rip through the pool house................................

DAMIEN

"Oh Damien this is so beautiful, I've never seen a more beautiful piece of stone before in my life" Damien was out of town on business,

But he did seek out some pleasure that could be doubled as help for he and his partner Jason. Damien and Katrina were taking their "Family Business" in another direction. They along with Monica and her husband Antonio, Jason and his wife Eve who had become a third partner in Katrina and Monica's Medical Practice, had all devised a plan that would guarantee all three families to wealth they never imagined was possible for them. Katrina, having witnessed the struggles her father endured while providing for his family, had vowed to never have her family suffer again due to weak financial situations.

Her Grandmother had been one of the wisest women she knew and had passed along some knowledge to Katrina before her death. Katrina had soaked up everything she could from Big Momma and vowed to always protect the family. Katrina, although the youngest had been, in Big Momma's eyes, the strongest when it came to the snake of the business world. Katrina had met Damien in her old neighborhood and gotten a vibe from him right away that he would be perfect for her future plans whatever they may have been. She herself did not know exactly how she was planning to look out for her family at such a young age, but she knew Damien Cunningham would be the perfect man to assist her when the time came. How right had she been and on this day Damien would prove just how right Katrina really was.

Damien and Jason had arrived in Kimberly, Cape Northern one of the most beautiful cities located in South Africa to embark on the beginning of the families' new venture. They were there to get the Allnatt Diamond, which rested in a large museum. The Allnatt was a beautiful stone that was given the name because of Major Ernest Allnatt who is believed to be one of the first holders of the precious gem. It measures in at 101.29 carats with a cushion cut and is rated the color fancy vivid yellow. Katrina had gained knowledge of the gem 6 months earlier and ran her idea around Damien first then her girlfriends. They all knew the great risk they would be taking but the benefits if success would prove to be well worth it. Damien started making trips over to the country to first see if the diamond was in fact in the museum then to see how the security worked at the building. He had made several trips over there in the course of five months and had started a romance with a beautiful lady by the name of Selma D'Anjou a native of the country. She would play a crucial part in what Damien had planned. The Allnatt diamond was worth $3 million dollars and each family stood to walk away with $1 million dollars. Damien and Jason had flown in earlier that morning while Antonio was already in the city waiting for them. The three men planned to do what they came to do as quickly as possible without error and get the hell out of dodge.

the most beautiful cities located in South Africa to embark on the beginning of the families' new venture.

The ring that rested on Damien's little conquest's finger was a replica of the Allnatt diamond and would aid the guys in their heist. Damien had given Selma a beautiful cushion cut diamond ring and was the most beautiful vivid color yellow. She was admiring the dazzling piece of jewelry and not believing that after only 4 months, Damien had purposed to her. She was so happy and could not wait to tell her family. Selma was so in love with Damien and even though it had only been a short time since they met, she knew they were made for each other.

"I was told that I must visit this lovely museum while I am visiting the city so how about you accompany me today my dear," Damien asked of the young lady.

"Sure, I would be honored to go with you and maybe later I can show you just how much I appreciate this beautiful ring," she gushed.

"Oh fa sho," Damien had slipped out of his mouth before he realized that he was not back home talking to one of the chicken heads that he would sneak away to have a fling with when he wasn't in Katrina's presence.

"Excuse me?" replied the beauty.

"I said for sure that will be something I have to look forward to my beautiful lady."

Damien planned to meet Jason there at 5:30 pm and Antonio who had been there for 3 hours already would throw the switch 15 minutes after their arrival, they would do their job and be gone by 8:00. They were going to be back on a plane headed back to the states by 11:00 that night. Antonio was already in place at the museum waiting for his partners in crime. Damien arrived with his lady friend on his arm at approximately 5:30 and began touring the museum. When they got to the diamond displays 15 minutes after their arrival, they heard a loud thump and the entire building went dark. People began running and screaming as Damien held on to his Selma's hand and telling her not to panic. All of a sudden she was snatched away from Damien and she felt someone pulling at her finger as she began to yell Damien's name. She kept screaming Damien's name all while swinging blindly in the darkness towards her assailant until she broke loose from them and started running in the direction from which she thought she had been snatched. She could hear Damien yelling her name telling her to stay put and he would find her. After what seemed like an eternity, but was only 5 minutes, the lights came back on and Damien looked around until he spotted Selma across the room coward on the floor in a fetal position. His eyes immediately went to her finger and smiled upon seeing that the ring he had given her was indeed on her finger. Poor Selma was a sniffling mess and they still couldn't leave right away due to a lock down in the museum. After the lights went out, the Authorities had to do a thorough inventory to make sure all of the merchandise was securely in their respective cases. Once the Authorities were satisfied all was well, they released the locks on the door and Damien took Selma back to her place to comfort her. They got back to her apartment and Damien insisted that she go and lay down while he fixed them some wine. As she was in her room thinking of the scare she had and thanking God for Damien, he was in the kitchen fixing two glasses of wine. He quickly dissolved 3 white pills into one of the glasses of wine and made his way back into the bedroom. Damien took the glass of tainted wine and handed it to Selma as he took the other glass.

"Here sweet heart, you drink your wine and I will go fix us a steak".

"No, please don't leave me just yet. Lay down with me Damien for just a little while,"

"Sure Selma, I can do whatever make you feel comfortable." Damien laid down with Selma as they listened to the sounds of Usher coming out the surround sound system. The two just sipped their wine while Damien held Selma close, each in their own thoughts.

"Damien whoever pulled me out of your grasp was pulling at my finger and I just knew they were trying to steal my ring, but when the lights came back on and I saw it on my finger, I was so relieved. Selma broke down even more with the thought of someone taking something so special away from her.

"Shhhh, baby don't you even worry about that ring because I can replace the ring, but you, I could never replace. Damien heard a slight snore and looked over to find Selma fast asleep. A smile crept onto Damien's face as he shook her to see if she would wake up. He took her hand and removed the ring as he continued to smile, but thinking that Jason, Antonio and he still had to get out of the country with the gem.

G

G had always wanted a Lamborghini and with the money he was sitting on he knew he could get one now. He also knew he would have too much explaining to do if he came up in a two hundred thousand dollar car. He laughed to himself as he imagined the looks on his Grandmother and Aunt's faces if he were to drive up in one of those. His mother would say very little he knew, because she had never been the nagging type, in fact she would alert her mother or sister of anything going on with her kids, but would tell them that she stay out of her kids affairs. Her favorite motto was, "They have to learn from their own mistakes." Granny Joe always told them they could hide nothing from her and would let them know every time she learned of something they were involved in. It baffled everyone how this lady could tell them everything they were doing, who they were with and what day it happened. Aunt Katrina just tried to prevent things from happening and wanted to force them to be somebody they were not. At least that was how they viewed her controlling nature.

G surmised that he only had three hundred thousand and would be foolish to spend it all on a car. When he thought about it, the money didn't sound like a lot. G decided he needed more money or at the very least a way to keep the money flowing. He knew of this dude named Rock and called him up to see if he could come thru and holla at him a little later. G then called Tyga and asked him what time was he coming out, "I'll be going over to granny Joe's in under an hour."

"I got something to run by you when you get here man", G said into the phone as he lit up a nicely rolled J. G had never sold weight before, but knew the money was good since he had some buddies that were into the game.

When Tyga made it to their grand-parent's house, he went in to see his mother and talked to her, and then he and G rode over to Rock's spot to holla at him. G filled Tyga in on what his plans were on the drive over, but told him that under no circumstances did he want Flex involved with this venture. They pulled up in their old stomping ground known as the infamous Dell Drive and drove slowly till they came to an old apartment complex that had seen better days. People were out and about with kids riding bikes and grills going and card games had the hood jumping. The young men made small talk with a few dudes they knew, but kept it moving right into the apartment complex. They got to a door and listened first, G turned around and asked Tyga was he strapped and Tyga nodded yes. G wasn't taking any chances around here and wanted to make sure his brother was not taking any either. They knocked on the door and waited for someone to answer, a woman that looked to be a crack whore answered with crusted white lips and smiling with yellowish teeth.

"Is Rock home?" G asked.

"Who wants to know?"

"Tell him G is here to see him."

"What you got for me if I let him know all of this?"

Tyga, who was no nonsense type of guy and not as nice as his brother sometimes, chuckled and replied in a slow country drawl, "What you think this is Let's Make A Deal? You better get your crack head ass out of my way before I throw your ass out the damn door."

"Tyga chill man," G whispered. Just then Rock came out of another room zipping his pants up, followed by another crack head female, "Y'all two got to roll up out of here, I got some business to take care of and here's your pay. Don't smoke it all up in one puff," Rock laughed as he tossed an eight ball in the women's direction. You would have thought they were chasing some flying money the awkward way they jumped to catch the drug and missing it only to fall in the floor wrestling to take ownership of this white gold.

"Bitch I was the one did all of that damn sucking for this shit not you,"

Well, bitch you done did your sucking, so it's my turn now to suck this glass di---."

"Get the hell out my house before I put foot in both y'all asses and take my shit back," The women broke the record getting up off the floor and getting the hell out that door, leaving the guys cracking the hell up.

"Fellas, what can I do for y'all?"

"Damn, you can't offer us anything to drink first?" Tyga asked only half joking.

"Naw man we straight," said G while giving Tyga a menacing look. Look man, we came to talk to you about getting some of that Glo and we'll be starting out with five Kilos."

"Shit, y'all got me confused for being a big dog when I'm just a squirrel trying to get a nut. I don't carry weight like that man and I don't

84

know who else does. Y'all boys starting kind of high, how much are you looking to spend off the bat?" *"These lil' dudes done turned five-O on me?"* thought Rock

"Yeah I see you ain't nothing but a squirrel tying to get a nut if you don't know the value of a Kilo?" Naw, now partna, ain't no need to get all bent out of shape over a simple question," Y'all dudes want some loud, I got some good stuff up in here."

Well he had just hit Tyga's number by offering up some smoke and he knew just what he was doing. He figured if these dudes had that kind of money to start out then he needed to get on their team. What was supposed to have been a meeting of the brothers starting up a business venture quickly turned into a partnership and a true friendship. The next person in line for G to see was going to be next to the hardest to convince. He knew he had to have a team of soldiers in place and thoroughly ready for inspection, he knew that each one of their backgrounds would be investigated. G knew if he didn't choose wisely, his chances at making this idea work would fall on deaf ears. The next couple of days, he along with Tyga and, Rock got together a team of five men they knew could be trusted and it was time for G to go see the person he knew could supply him with what he needed.

"Mr. Grey, you have a guest to see you," Geoff's secretary buzzed his office to let him know someone was there to see him.

"I have meetings this morning Sylvia and I don't see people without an appointment." Sylvia was a pretty girl with no common sense about her, but then everyone knew Geoff didn't hire her for her head. It was strictly for the satisfaction of his head and not the big head. "There's a good looking young gentleman to see you and he says you are his uncle."

"Send him right in Sylvia."

"Hey Unc, thanks for seeing me."

"G, you know you never thank me for seeing you. What can I do for you Nephew? Your mom is not having any outside issues is she?"

"Naw, she's doing the same as she was the last time you saw her. she has a little cold right now, but other than that she is good."

"Oh okay, what you up for then Nephew?"

"Do you have time to go to breakfast with your Nephew? My treat." Geoff loved to eat and his Nephew knew to get him in a comfortable setting for this particular conversation.

"What are we waiting for then son, let's get going."

Geoff and G were seated at a nearby diner and G had told his Uncle what he wanted to dabble into and of course he had to fully explain to his Uncle how things would run and promise him to never let word get back to the family about what he was doing. Geoff told him he would fully train him on how to look after himself and he and Tyga both would have to work for him in the construction business as well to have legitimate employment.

86

"Well Unc, we were discussing starting a car dealership together. We figured Aunt Katrina could talk to Mr. Andreas and see if he would offer some business advice on how to get started."

"I see you boys have really thought this thing through and you don't have to bother your Aunt, I can talk to Andreas for you today and get with you this evening at momma's house. You know damn well if you bring anything up to Katrina, you will have to do a lot more convincing her than me"

"Alright Unc, see you then." Unknown to G, he had been followed all morning and his tail would continue to follow him until the moment was right.

Damien

Damien, Jason and Antonio met up at Cape Town International Airport and were eagerly awaiting their departure flight. Damien was a bundle of nerves, although he tried not to show it and was ready to just get the hell out of the country. The countless trips he had made to the Country were really starting to wear on him, but if he could just get out this one last time without problems from customs, then he wouldn't have to worry about coming back again. They had successfully attained the Allnatt Diamond and the hard part was almost over, getting it out of the country.

"Damien where did you stash the gem man?" Jason asked. I got it right in here, Damien said patting his jacket pocket. "Damien, do you think that is smart to carry something that valuable in such an obvious place?"

"Do you have a better idea Antonio?" Damien was running on empty, this trip had his adrenalines on high alert, but he was truly running on empty right now. His buddies saw this and Jason asked the guys to follow him. The guys all stepped outside and around the building into an alleyway. They knew they had two hours to wait for their flight. "Let me see the gem Damien." Jason stated.

"Are you trying to say you do not trust me Jason?" Damien did not like the way this was sounding at all and the look on his face gave all his emotions away, not that he was trying to hide how he felt about his loyalty being tested.

"Damien, man come on don't go there with me. You are tired man is all and not thinking rationally or you would have known not to even think about walking through those monitors with that gem in your pocket. I know how we can get it through with no trouble." Damien and Antonio looked at each other and asked simultaneously, "How is that?"

"I'm going to swallow it."

"Man I had not thought about that, that's pure genius." Damien reached into his pocket and passed the gem around to the guys so both could get a feel of the precious stone. "There's a deli right beside the airport, let's go there and order something to eat so you can coat your stomach good before you take it down." suggested Antonio. The guys came out of the alleyway and headed back towards Cape Town International all feeling more secure with their decision on how to get the gem out of the country. They knew they were working with very little time to get some food ordered and get back inside the terminal in time to catch their flight. They were seated quickly and ordered right away as they had a drink while waiting for their food order. The cute little waitress brought some complimentary rolls and water to the table while they waited for the food to come. The guys looked at the bread, then at each other and smiled widely as they knew they were all thinking the same thing. Jason took the stone and tossed it into his mouth with a big gulp of water and swallowed. He then took some bread and began eating big pieces as he chased this all with big gulps of water. When he began to have trouble breathing.

"Whoa, slow down my friend before you over do things," Damien stated. Antonio noticed that Jason really was having a hard time breathing and asked if he was okay. Jason could only shake his head from side to side. "Damn man, I think he is choking on the diamond," Antonio stated as he jumped from his seat to help his friend. Damien went to help, but looked up just in time to see a familiar man pointing in his direction. "Oh shit, that's Selma's brother coming this way."

Grey Family Home

"Mama, is Katrina coming over here today?" Deborah asked of her mother.

"I don't know, but I'll call and ask her for you."

"Can I do anything for you in the meantime?"

"No ma'am." Deborah replied weakly. She didn't want to alarm her mom, but she had been having trouble breathing all day and would just feel better if her sister would come over. Mama Joe went to call her youngest daughter and while she was trying to reach Katrina, Thomas came in to talk with his oldest daughter and see how her day was going.

"Hey Deb, how are you today?"

"I'm doing alright daddy," Deb stated with a slight smile.

"Well I'm glad to hear you say that sweetheart, but you know you do not have to be strong for daddy now."

"I know Daddy, but I am doing better than some days although not as good as other days." Thomas sat down in a chair beside his daughter's bed and grabbed her petite hand.

"That sounds like a more truthful answer.

"Daddy I am so scared."

"I know sweetheart. I am also and I really wish I could take that fear away from you, but I can't. What I can do is hold you in my arms and ask God to replace that fear with courage. Baby girl, I have never been a man of tears or fears, but I have never been a man with an ill child either. We have to all become stronger for you and not ask God why because even though we don't understand his reasoning, mistakes are never made coming from him."

Thomas just held his daughter in his arms as he rocked her with tears in his eyes. Mama Joe was about to come and let Deborah know she didn't reach Katrina, but backed out of the room upon seeing this touching moment. Mama Joe could not believe Katrina could be so careless as to not be around a phone when she knew they would need her at any moment. She picked the phone up to dial Katrina again and just as she was waiting for the phone to ring, Thomas called his wife's name in a panicked stated. Mama Joe threw the phone down and ran to Deborah's room to see that her daughter had passed out in her husband's arms. She rushed to his side filled with fear and panic as she grabbed her daughter in her arms as she rocked her back and fourth. Bridgette came in the room upon hearing all of the yelling and although she was usually composed in these situations, she completely lost it as she looked and saw her grandparents surrounding her mother. Mama no!!!!!!!!!!!!!!!!!!!!!!!

Made in the USA
Columbia, SC
30 September 2020